Margaret Tudor, Queen of Scots

The Life of King Henry VIII's Sister

Margaret Tudor, Queen of Scots

The Life of King Henry VIII's Sister

Sarah-Beth Watkins

Winchester, UK
Washington, USA

First published by Chronos Books, 2017
Chronos Books is an imprint of John Hunt Publishing Ltd., Laurel House, Station Approach,
Alresford, Hants, SO24 9JH, UK
office1@jhpbooks.net
www.johnhuntpublishing.com

For distributor details and how to order please visit the 'Ordering' section on our website.

ISBN: 978 1 78535 676 6
978 1 78535 677 3 (ebook)
Library of Congress Control Number: 2017931223

A CIP catalogue record for this book is available from the British Library.

Cover image by kind permission of the Royal Collection Trust/ (copyright symbol) Her Majesty
Queen Elizabeth II 2017.

Design: Stuart Davies

Printed and bound by CPI Group (UK) Ltd, Croydon, CR0 4YY, UK

We operate a distinctive and ethical publishing philosophy in all
areas of our business, from our global network of authors to
production and worldwide distribution.

CONTENTS

Books by Sarah-Beth Watkins

Catherine of Braganza
The Tudor Brandons
Lady Katherine Knollys: The Unacknowledged Daughter of
King Henry VIII
Ireland's Suffragettes

Books for Writers:
Telling Life's Tales
Life Coaching for Writers
The Lifestyle Writer
The Writer's Internet

Chapter One

The Early Years
1489–1502

The old palace of Westminster was alive with the news that King Henry VII's queen had given birth to a healthy daughter. Following the birth of their first child Prince Arthur in 1486 the king had hoped for another son but no matter, they were still young and more children would follow. Lady Margaret Beaufort, the king's mother, had taken charge of the queen's lying-in. A formidable force in the early Tudor court, she had even written a set of protocols for Arthur's birth that set out exactly how a royal child should be brought into the world.

Lady Margaret ensured Elizabeth of York had spent nearly a month in confinement surrounded by hangings of 'riche Clothe of blew Arras, with Flourdeliffis of Golde'[1] and with a bed and pallet covered by a canopy of gold cloth embroidered with the red roses of Lancaster. All the tapestries depicted flowers and symbols, no images of people were allowed lest they scare the queen during labour. In a time where superstition was rife, religious relics adorned a small altar to guarantee a smooth birth and with all the preparations made, Elizabeth was safely delivered of an auburn-haired princess at nine o'clock in the evening on 29 November 1489. The baby's grandmothers, Lady Margaret and Elizabeth Wydeville, were in attendance as Margaret Tudor came into the world, aided by a midwife, Alice Massey, who was paid a handsome £10 (around £4800) for her services.

This new daughter of the now joined Houses of Lancaster and York was baptised on the feast day of St Andrew – an auspicious omen for one whose life would become entwined with Scotland. Wrapped cosily against the winter chill, Margaret knew nothing of her future as officers of arms led the procession from the queen's chamber to the chapel at Westminster. Anne Fiennes, Marchioness of Berkeley, carried the little princess, escorted by the Earls of Arundel and Shrewsbury, closely followed by Queen Elizabeth's sister Anne, holding the baby's richly laced chrisom. Many more nobles escorted them including Viscount Wells carrying a gold salt cellar and the Earl of Kent with a pair of gilt basins, gifts for the new princess.

They were met at the chapel by John Alcock, Bishop of Ely, who baptised the baby Margaret in the impressive silver font loaned from Canterbury Cathedral that had been lined with fine linen cloth of Rennes, watched by her godparents; her grandmother Lady Margaret, the Duchess of Norfolk, the Archbishop of Canterbury and the Earl of Shrewsbury. Over 120 torches were lit and the little chapel suddenly blazed with light. As trumpets sounded, Margaret was taken back to her room and settled into her oak cradle padded with ermine and covered with a canopy of cloth of gold, to be looked after by her personal governess Lady Guildford, nurse Alice Davy, two cradle rockers Anne Maylande and Margaret Troughton, and Alice Bywymble, her 'day-wife'. Oblivious to the fussing around her the new princess slipped back into sleep.

These early days were spent in the sprawling rooms at the old palace of Westminster until an outbreak of the measles forced the court to move to Greenwich for the Christmas season, and Margaret was soon moved to her own nursery in at Sheen, a favourite residence of her father's next to the Thames. For the time being the nursery belonged to her alone. Her older brother, the three-year-old Arthur, newly created Prince of Wales and heir to the throne, had his own household at Farnham Palace in Surrey and even though they were raised apart he would always have a soft spot for his younger sister.

Margaret was a child adored by her family but her mother was often ill or pregnant as she was growing up. The princess became closer to her father who although appearing as a stern and strict monarch showed affection for a child who would come to share his love of music and hunting. Lady Margaret Beaufort, the princess's namesake and grandmother, took charge of her day-to-day care and education, hoping her granddaughter would grow up to be as pious and educated as herself. This remarkable woman and mother of Henry VII had fought for long hard years for her son to be placed on the throne. Now in her later years she often took charge at court organising the queen's other laying-ins and standing in for her while she was indisposed.

Margaret's mother doted on her and made frequent trips to the nursery when she could, but Elizabeth was confined again for the birth of her next child, this time at Greenwich, in June 1491. At the end of the month, Henry Tudor was born and a sumptuous nursery was prepared at Eltham for both of the younger royal siblings. They were joined in 1492 by the Princess Elizabeth, born in July at Sheen. Henry came to dominate the nursery, overindulged by the all-female staff who doted on him. He was the spoilt younger brother whom everyone loved and adored, annoying and amusing his older sister in equal measure.

No longer fussed over, Margaret still had her chance to shine. At a three-day celebratory joust held in honour of Henry's creation as Duke of York in 1494, she had her first official public role giving out the prizes. The knights undertook 'the said enterprise, specially for the pleasure of their redoubted lady and fairest young princess'[2] who, soon to be five, handed out diamond and ruby rings to the victors handed to her by her mother's ladies, Elizabeth Stafford, Anne Percy and Anne Neville.

Little Elizabeth was kept in the nursery too ill and too young to be out in public. In September she died of a wasting disease and the nursery was all the quieter for Margaret and Henry. Their parents held an extravagant funeral befitting the little royal costing around £150,000 in today's money and she was buried in state at Westminster Abbey. Her loss was felt keenly but the nursery soon had a new occupant. Princess Mary was born on 18 March 1496 and joined her older brother and sister. Two other children Edward born in 1500 and Edmund possibly born in 1501 did not survive infancy.

Life in the nursery wasn't all play for the older siblings. Margaret had her grandmother to educate her in how to be a great lady and her mother Elizabeth also played her part teaching the Tudor princess how to read and write. She also had the benefit of Henry's tutors and could listen in on his lessons – if she felt inclined to. Henry was provided with excellent tuition; the poet laureate John Skelton was employed around 1496 to teach him grammar and Latin and over time he was also tutored by Giles d'Ewes in French and music. John Holt and William Hone added to his general education but whereas Henry soaked up knowledge and learning, Margaret had little time for it. According to Strickland, Margaret 'was neither a learned nor an educated princess'[3] but she was becoming an accomplished lady.

Tudor princesses were never brought up to reign so what need did Margaret have to study as seriously as her younger brother? As she grew older, she knew that the most important thing she could do for her father's kingdom was to marry well. Henry VII wished for peace with Scotland, then linked to England's age-old enemy France through their 'auld alliance' and a constant source of turmoil. The marriage negotiations for Margaret to wed their king, James IV, although started in 1495, were to go through years of ups and downs as would England's relationship with Scotland. Henry's counsellors weren't keen on the idea to begin with but the king won them over, stating 'Supposing that all my male progeny should become extinct, and the kingdom devolve by law to Margaret's heirs, will England be damaged thereby and not rather benefited? For since it ever happens that the less becomes subservient to the greater, the accession will be that of Scotland to England, and not of England to Scotland'.[4] His words would underline the tensions between the two countries for many years to come.

Born in 1473, Margaret's intended husband James IV was the son of James III, who had been killed after the Battle of Sauchieburn, a rebellion to overthrow his rule and place the young James on the throne. James III was believed to have survived the battle but being injured fled on horse and asked for assistance at Milltown near Bannockburn. A priest was called but being one of the rebels, he drove his dagger into the king's heart, killing him outright. James blamed himself for his father's death – he had sided with the rebels led by the 1st Lord Home but ordered that his father not be hurt during the battle – and wore an iron belt afterwards in penance to which he added an extra link every year, spending much time on pilgrimage and aiding charity work for his atonement.

Still, James IV was crowned on 24 June 1488; an athletic, energetic king who took to his duties vigorously, travelling around his kingdom constantly, meeting his people and quelling any uprisings. He loved jousting, hunting, hawking, music and poetry, and spoke several different languages. Education was important to him and in 1496 he passed an education act for noble sons to learn Latin and law. He took an interest in medicine and dentistry, even paying a poor unfortunate to practice pulling his teeth! He even embroidered and undertook fine needlework in the evenings – a hyperactive king who hated to keep still.

The negotiations for his marriage to Margaret stalled when James gave refuge to Perkin Warbeck who claimed he was Queen Elizabeth's brother, one of the princes in the tower, and the rightful heir to the English throne. Warbeck had garnered support throughout Europe and Scotland welcomed him much to Henry VII's annoyance. James gave him a place close to court, new clothes and even a bride, Lady Katherine Gordon, daughter of the Earl of Huntly. For James, Warbeck was nothing more than a pawn in his ploy to reach a better agreement with the Spanish, who would soon send their daughter Catherine of Aragon to marry Prince Arthur and wished to see both countries at peace. James wanted to ally himself with Spain and angled for a Spanish bride but there was none to give. Not to be put off and eager for their kingdoms to be in harmony, Henry VII sent ambassadors to continue negotiations for a marriage to Margaret. The Scottish king was infuriated. He felt Margaret was too young to marry and it would be years before she would produce any heirs.

Henry had hoped it would bring their two countries peace but James wasn't ready to agree to a treaty without a fight – literally. He gathered his army to invade England and after crossing the River Tweed 'laid waste the fields, pillaged and then burnt the houses and villages. The natives who resisted he cruelly killed…having widely devastated the countryside of Northumberland, he would have gone even further but for his troops being so laden with spoils that they refused to follow him'.[5] Warbeck, who had been invited to ride with the king, protested at his mistreatment of the English people – those he claimed as his own – and left for Ireland.

In May 1497, when England and Scotland were still enmeshed in hostilities, Henry VII had to recall his troops to focus on the Cornish rebellion that saw 15,000 rebels march towards the capital. Margaret was hustled to the safety of the Tower of London with her mother and siblings as the mob grew closer. They were subdued at the Battle of Blackheath, but Warbeck, seeing that the Cornish men shared no loyalty to the crown, took his opportunity and arrived near Land's End in September with a small army of 120 men to march on London. Gathering more men under his banner on the way, the rebels didn't get far before they heard that the king's army was closing in on them. Warbeck deserted at Taunton and headed for the sanctuary of Beaulieu Abbey in Hampshire where after being offered a pardon, he was captured and taken to the Tower. He would be executed two years later and his claims to the English throne would amount to nothing.

Both James IV and Henry VII now looked for a lasting peace between their kingdoms. In September 1497 the Treaty of Ayton, a seven-year truce, was agreed. James IV's commissioner Pedro de Ayala from Spain was then sent to England to negotiate further terms and to extend the truce to the lifetime of the longest living king plus one year. Should further hostilities arise, Spain was charged with mediating between the two countries thus ensuring a peaceful and undivided nation for their daughter, Catherine of Aragon, to marry into.

There was also another marriage to go back to arranging but Henry VII now showed more concern for the welfare of his daughter. As both his mother and his queen pointed out she was still far too young. Henry's mother Lady Margaret Beaufort had experienced a horrific labour with him at the age of 13 and was so damaged from childbirth she could never have any more children. This marriage however would seal the new peace and although Princess Margaret was only seven, preparations could be made. James was 16 years older than her and Henry told the Spanish ambassador, Pedro Ayala, 'The Queen and my mother are very much against the marriage. They say if the marriage were concluded we should be obliged to send the princess directly to Scotland, in which case they fear the King of Scotland would not wait, but injure her and endanger her health'.[6]

They could delay until she was older but in the meantime still ensure that once Margaret was of age there would be no objections. Papal dispensation was required and sought as James and Margaret were distant cousins through James's great grandmother, Lady Jane Beaufort, granddaughter of John of Gaunt – also Lady Margaret's ancestor.

Margaret and her father received a positive reply to their request from Pope Alexander VI.

... you, the first-born daughter of our dearest son in Christ, Henry, the illustrious King of England, being now about ten and a half years of age, cannot contract marriage with our dearest son in Christ, James, illustrious King of Scotland, according to the desire of the said King James, to whom you are related in the third and fourth degree of consanguinity and affinity, unless the authority of the apostolic see be granted for this; we wishing fitly to provide thereupon, inclining to your applications on this behalf, by our apostolic authority and of certain knowledge, by the tenor of these present letters, as a gift of special favour, grant a dispensation to you and the said King James, freely and lawfully to contract matrimony together from this time forth, and to remain therein when it shall have been contracted[7]

In time Margaret's nuptials would be arranged, but first there was the joining of Henry VII and Elizabeth of York's first born and his Spanish princess to celebrate. Catherine of Aragon had arrived at Plymouth on 2 October 1501 after an arduous sea voyage. At one point the storms were so bad the ship had to return to Spain until the wind died down. Catherine had been violently sea sick but when they sailed again, the journey took just five days and the princess was welcomed by people thronging the streets as she travelled towards London and her new life.

There was great rejoicing for Prince Arthur and Catherine's wedding on 14 November at St Paul's Cathedral. The young Henry had had the privilege of escorting Catherine into London two days previously and dressed in white satin, was in place to give the bride away to his brother. After the ceremony there were days of feasting, jousts and entertainments. Margaret and Henry took to the floor one evening showing off their dancing skills, until Henry stole the show by flinging off 'his gown, and danced in his jacket with the said Lady Margaret, in so goodly and pleasant a manner, that it was to the king and queen great and singular pleasure' (Leland). They were also watched by some special guests at the wedding who had a great significance to Margaret – the Scottish ambassadors who had been commissioned 'to marry her at once, as might be most convenient and advisable'.[8]

James had sent his trusted men; the Archbishop of Glasgow, the Earl of Bothwell and the Bishop of Moray to conclude marriage negotiations with the English councillors the Archbishop of Canterbury, Bishop of Winchester and Thomas Howard, the Earl of Surrey. Although the Scottish king wanted to marry as soon as possible they were charged to agree that the wedding would not take place before 1 September 1503, giving Margaret time to grow into adolescence at least.

There was much to be agreed upon. Margaret's dowry would include what palace and lands would become hers including Linlithgow Palace, Stirling Castle and the rents from the Ettrick Estate. As Queen of Scotland she would be endowed with a personal yearly income of £500 and James was to provide for her 24 English servants, plus finance the 'apparatus of her body, the ornamenting of her residences, her vehicles, stud, furniture, utensils, food, dress, private and domestic affairs, and all other things whatsoever, necessary and becoming the honour, state, rank, and dignity of the said Lady Margaret'.[9] In return James would receive 30,000 golden nobles (around £10,000 or £35,000 Scots) paid over three years with the first instalment to accompany Margaret on her wedding journey. The Tudor princess was to be kept in the luxury she was so accustomed to.

Once all was decided, the marriage treaty was signed on 24 January 1502 and the very next day Margaret and James were betrothed with the Earl of Bothwell standing in for the Scottish king at Richmond Palace, newly restored and renamed after the 1497 fire which had destroyed the previous wooden palace of Sheen and Margaret's early nursery. The new palace was a fitting venue showing off Henry VII's wealth and prosperity. Built of red brick and white stone, it was a magnificent sight with its octagonal towers capped with pepper-pot cupolas and ornate brass weathervanes situated in sculpted gardens by the riverside.

High Mass was first held in the chapel with the King, Queen, Prince Henry, Princess Mary, Princess Margaret and the Scottish ambassadors present as well as many peers, lords and ladies of court dressed in their finest clothes. In the Queen's Great Chamber afterwards, the ceremony took place with the archbishop starting the proceedings by asking the king, queen and Margaret if they knew of any impediment to the marriage. Each declared there was none. He then inquired whether Margaret came to the betrothal of her own free will to which she replied 'if it please my lord and father the King and my lady mother the Queen'[10] and knelt for her parent's blessing.

Margaret and the Earl of Bothwell then stood before her parents, sister and brother surrounded by the new emblem of the Tudor rose and Scottish thistle entwined, as the Archbishop of Glasgow then turned to the Scottish representatives and queried 'whether it was the will and mind of the King of Scots, and full intent, that the said Earl of Bothwell should in his name, assure the said princess'[11] to which they agreed. The Earl of Bothwell took his cue to give his marriage vow on behalf of James IV.

> *I, Patrick, Earl of Bothwell, procurator of the right excellent, right high and mighty prince, James, by the grace of God King of Scotland, my sovereign lord, having suifficient authority, power and commandment to contract matrimony per verba de presenti, in the name of, and for my said sovereign lord, with thee, Margaret, the first begotten daughter of the right excellent, right high and mighty prince and princess, Henry, by the grace of God King of England, and Elizabeth, queen of the same, as by the procuratory of my said sovereign lord, at this present time openly read and published, more plainly appears by virtue of the same procuratory, and as procurator of my said sovereign lord, James, King of Scotland, and in his name*

and behalf, and by his special commandment, contract matrimony with thee, Margaret, and take thee into and for the wife and spouse of my said sovereign lord, James, King of Scotland, and all other for thee (as procurator foresaid) forsake, during his and thine lives natural, and thereto, as procurator foresaid, I plight and give thee his faith and truth, by power and authority foresaid committed and given to me.[12]

Margaret responded:

I, Margaret, the first-begotten daughter of the right excellent, right high and mighty prince and princess, Henry, by the grace of God King of England, and Elizabeth, queen of the same, wittingly and of deliberate mind, having twelve years complete in age, in the month of November last past, contract matrimony with the right excellent, right high and mighty prince, James, King of Scotland, and the person of whom, Patrick, Earl of Bothwell, procurator of the said prince, James, King of Scotland, [represents] and take the said James, King of Scotland, unto and for my husband and spouse, and all other for him forsake, during his and mine lives natural, and thereto I plight and give to him, in your person as procurator foresaid, my faith and truth.[13]

The ceremony over, trumpets resounded around the palace and 'a loud noise of minstrels played'.[14] A sumptuous feast was enjoyed by all, Margaret especially, as now she sat with her mother at the top table as Queen of Scotland. Her brother Henry was so furious he was reported to have cried tears of frustration. This young prince who was so self-important and had ruled over Margaret in their childhood days was thoroughly put out by his sister's elevation.

In later years, the proxy marriage was immortalised in a history of Henry VII's reign by the poet Charles Aleyn:

Margaret, eldest daughter of the king,
King James to wife did by a proxy take,
Which, told by fame, the bells contend to ring
A peal as loud as fame's; and bonfires make
So great a light that if heaven's light were done,
They might have made a day without a sun.[15]

As the celebrations continued at the palace, with feasting, disguisings and jousts over three days, so too did the people of London rejoice. A proclamation of the marriage was read out at St Paul's Cross and Te Deums sung around the city. Bonfires were lit and Henry VII, although renowned for his stinginess, provided barrels of wine for his people's celebrations. Margaret was in her element as the new Queen of Scotland and queen of the jousts. Wrapped up in her resplendent furs against the January cold she presided over a tournament held in her honour on the afternoon of her betrothal. The Duke of Buckingham led the joust wearing out one horse and swopping it for a charger richly dressed in blue and crimson velvet. Amongst the challengers was also a newcomer, the dashing Charles Brandon, who would later come to feature in her sister Princess Mary's life.

The next morning Margaret, 'by the voice of the principal officer of arms' thanked the gathered nobles who had taken 'pains and charge'[16] to joust for her sake and gave out rewards to the victors. First prize was awarded to Lord William Courtenay, her uncle by marriage. More feasting followed and a pageant was staged for Margaret's entertainment that included a 'curious building with fenestrailles, or windows, brilliantly illuminated, out of which stepped forth, in pairs, several morris-dancers'.[17]

Exhausted but loving every minute, Margaret presided over another joust the following day and sat with her parents for a 'notable supper'[18] after which Henry VII gave gifts to the Scottish ambassadors who were returning to their homeland. The Archbishop of Glasgow received a cup of gold, 6 great standing silver cups, 24 silver bowls, a silver basin and ewer with the Earl of Bothwell also receiving similar gifts. The Bishop of Moray was gifted a gold cup and a crimson velvet bag full of gold coins. All richly rewarded for the part they played in negotiating Margaret's marriage to their king.

James IV meanwhile was preparing for his bride's eventual arrival. A new palace was being built for her next to the old Holyrood Abbey in Edinburgh, founded in 1128. Since then the abbey had been an important centre of activity for Scottish royals who often stayed in its guesthouse. James now ordered the construction of a magnificent Gothic home for his betrothed to include a great hall, chapel, gallery and royal apartments – Margaret's in the south range and James's in the west.

In England, Margaret had her own new apartments for the time being at Windsor and Westminster and here she dreamed of the life that was ahead of her. She revelled in her new title and the honour and respect she now received at court, and wondered what life would be like in Scotland with the handsome if much older James. James hardly spared a thought for Margaret, his marriage to her would make Scotland richer and bring peace between the two countries but he was not interested in her as a woman. She was still a child and would serve as mother to his legitimate children in time. For now Janet Kennedy was keeping his bed warm; one of a long line of mistresses including Marion Boyd, Isabel Stewart and Margaret Drummond. Lady Drummond had been a special favourite of James's and it had been rumoured that they might even have secretly married. The Spanish ambassador, Pedro de Ayala certainly wrote that James 'was keeping a great lady with great state in a castle, he visited her from time to time. Afterwards he sent her to the house of her father, who is a knight and married her'[19] but there is no recorded evidence for any marriage to the lady. In 1501 she died after dining, along with her sisters Eupheme and Sibylla, supposedly of food poisoning. It was a terrible tragedy and one not wholly believed by several factions who spun conspiracy theories out of the poor girls' demise. Had someone poisoned them intentionally? We will never know but James was devastated at his mistress's death. His one consolation was their daughter Margaret born in 1497, who added to his other children, amounted to six illegitimate offspring by four different mothers with another one on the way to be born in July 1502.

But the new Queen of Scotland was completely unaware of James's mistresses and their progeny. For Margaret, 1502 was the year of growing up. Queen Elizabeth's Privy Purse expenses show Margaret's love for fine clothes, dance and music. Payments were made for the furring of a crimson gown, the making of a black velvet one and several pairs of sarcenet sleeves in white, orange and black. One Henry Roper was also commissioned to bring pewters basins, washing bowls, a pair of bellows and a fire pan for Margaret's use in her apartments. She learned to play the lute and clavichord at an early age and we see further payments of strings for her lute paid to the music teacher she shared with her brother, Giles d'Ewes, and payments to her own group of minstrels for her entertainment.

Sadly, one of the payments was for mourning clothes. In April 1502, Margaret's older brother Prince Arthur died. Arthur and Catherine had been living in Ludlow in a damp, cold castle positioned high above the River Teme, near the border of Wales. Catherine had hated every minute of living there whilst Arthur saw it as his duty as Lord Warden of the Marches, responsible for security along the border. Disease, probably the sweating sickness, had come to the area in the early months of 1502 and no one was safe from 'a malign vapour which proceeded from the air'[20] including the royal couple.

A messenger arrived at court on 4th April after riding hard for two days from Ludlow and informed the Privy Council of the terrible tragedy that had befallen the heir to the throne. The King's confessor, a Friar Observant, was chosen to deliver the news to Henry VII. Clearing the room, he informed his king that his son had passed away. Henry immediately sent for the queen and together they clung to one another overcome with grief. Elizabeth tried to stay strong and reminded her husband 'God has left you yet a fair Prince, two Princesses and God is where he was and we are both young enough'.[21] As soon as she was back in her own apartments her strength failed her and she wept uncontrollably until her ladies sent for the king. The court was plunged into mourning so soon after the celebrations for Margaret's marriage. As the prince's body was being prepared for his coffin, dirges were sung in St Paul's Cathedral and across the churches in London. This was one death they could not have foreseen and England was in shock.

After Arthur's burial at Worcester Cathedral, his 16-year-old widow returned to court. Pale and fragile, Catherine had been ill as well but unlike Arthur had surprisingly managed to shake off the usually fatal sickness. The prince's death brought the family closer together and Catherine now lodged at Durham House and spent many hours with the Tudor princesses, Margaret and Mary. Queen Elizabeth's health was also poor and she was in the early stages of pregnancy again so the girls spent their summer quietly together, still numb from their loss.

Arthur's death meant Margaret was now second in the succession and the ten-year-old Henry was first in line to become the next King of England, but it was Margaret that Arthur remembered the most in his will. She was left his jewels, plate, gowns and robes although it would be many years before she received them. Her brother would make sure of that.

Henry VII

Chapter Two

Marriage to James IV
1503

On 2 February 1503 Margaret's mother went into premature labour whilst at the Tower of London for Candlemas. Queen Elizabeth attended church in the morning trying to ignore the nagging sensation in her lower back but by the afternoon her birth pains were coming on strong. She had hoped to have the child, her eighth, at Richmond but there was no time. Fortunately her midwife, Alice Massey, was by her side to assist the delivery as the queen's apartments were hastily arranged for a lying-in. Taking to her bed, Elizabeth had the most arduous and painful labour but was finally delivered of a baby daughter, Katherine.

Nine days later Elizabeth died on her 37th birthday probably from postpartum infection. Henry VII was inconsolable and shut himself away from his court to grieve in private. He spared no expense on her state funeral at Westminster Abbey, spending the equivalent of over £1,000,000 in today's money. Margaret, Henry and Mary, so recently devastated by their brother's death, were plunged into mourning again. Sadly their new sibling survived just a few weeks.

Margaret had become particularly close to her mother since her betrothal, and her death hit her hard. She would soon be leaving for Scotland so they had been making the most of their time left together, attending Mass and appearing at court. Thomas More wrote a touching elegy to Elizabeth which included a reference to her daughter:

Farewell, my daughter, Lady Margaret.
God wot full oft it grieved hath my mind,

That ye should go where we should seldom meet;
Now am I gone and have left you behind,
O mortal folk that we be very blind,
What we least fear, full oft it is most nigh.
From you depart I first, and lo! now here I lie.[1]

In May the king was roused from his grief to send commissioners to Scotland to arrange the handover of Margaret's dower lands including 'the forest of Etrick, the whole county of Mar, the domains of Dunbar and Coldbrandspath, excepting Dunbar Castle, the palace and domain of Linlithgow, the castle and domain of Stirling, the palace and domain of Methven, the castle and domain of Downe in Perthshire, and the earldom of Monteith'.[2] With the legalities being confirmed, Lady Margaret Beaufort took charge of her granddaughter's departure for Scotland. The princess's trousseau needed completing. There were gowns to be made and cloths to be embroidered. The needlewomen were made busy by the making of regal purple and cloth of gold gowns amongst others and kirtles, smocks, petticoats and hose. There were shoes to be made to match each gown. Livery was needed in green and black for her litter-bearers and green cloth of gold and white for her footmen. Her litter itself was to be covered with cloth of gold and embroidered with the royal coat of arms. The Tudor arms was painted on her coach too and if she felt she wished to ride she had a saddle embroidered with tiny red roses to sit upon her palfrey. Henry VII, notorious for being mean, again spent a fortune in making sure that Margaret had everything to start her new life and show off the wealth of the Tudors to the poorer Scots.

On 27 June, Henry VII escorted Margaret as far as her grandmother's home at Collyweston which had been prepared in advance to cater for the huge entourage that would accompany her on her journey north. Lady Beaufort had changed the once simple manor house in Northamptonshire into a palace fit for a queen with a 'chapel, library, counting-house, great parlour, Queen's chamber, guest-chambers, a jewel-house, vestry, wardrobe of the beds, wardrobe of robes, spicery, brewery, bake-house, pastrye kitchen and scollere, a skaldyng-house, wette larder, and many other rooms, besides a clock-house in the great tower'.[3] A new guest house had been built for the occasion, the gardens and ponds tidied and a summerhouse installed for their pleasure.

Margaret spent her last idyllic days there with her family, conscious that she may never see them again. Once she was in Scotland there would be no reason to travel back to her father's court and like many a princess who married into another country, she was excited, scared and anxious all in equal measure. She had lost so much lately with her brother and mother's death that it was heart-wrenching to say goodbye to her grandmother, her siblings and her father. Henry VII must have felt it too. She was his favourite daughter and at their final parting, he gave her his blessing and a beautifully illuminated *Book of Hours*. Inside he had written 'Remember yr kynde and loving fader in y good prayers'. Then further in the book, on the blank page opposite prayers for December, he wrote 'Pray for your louving fader, that gave you thys booke, and I gyve you at all tymes godd's blessyng and myne. HENRY R'.[4]

On 8 July Margaret left Collyweston to start her new life. In charge of the procession was the Earl of Surrey, Treasurer of England, and his wife, the Countess of Surrey, acting as Margaret's chaperone. Margaret was 'very nobly accompanied, in fair order and array, of the said Lords, Knights, Ladies and others'.[5] The Somerset Herald, John Yonge, lists all those that accompanied her and recorded each day's events for his chronicle. There was absolute precision to the magnificent cavalcade. The Earl of Surrey led the way with the court nobles and a military type vanguard of knights. Margaret set out, dressed in velvet and cloth of gold, behind her standard-bearer,

Sir Davey Owen, surrounded by her liveried footmen, an extra palfrey led by her Master of Horse, Thomas Wortley, and her litter for if she tired of riding. Her richly dressed ladies followed on horseback with the more elderly ladies in carriages surrounded by squires and servants to do their bidding. Musicians and minstrels accompanied them for their entertainment and to announce Margaret's arrival in each town they passed so that their sheriffs and officials were forewarned to ride out to greet them. This immense and slow-moving procession meant it would take her over a month to reach Scotland.

Her route first took her through Grantham, Newark, Tuxford, Doncaster, Pontefract, Tadcaster, and then to York. All along the way the roads were lined with people to wish her well and wave her on, scattering flowers in her path and 'bringing great vessels full of drink, and giving the same to them that need had of it'.[6] Before York, Yonge recorded how splendid Henry Percy, the 5th Earl of Northumberland, looked as he rode out to greet Margaret with 400 of his men 'upon a fair courser, with a footcloth to the ground of crimson velvet...his arms very rich in many places upon his saddle and harness, his stirrups gilt, himself arrayed of a gown of the said crimson. At the openings of his sleeves and the collar, a great border of stones (jewels)'[7] and he even wore black velvet boots. Not to be outdone, Margaret ordered the procession to stop so that she could change into her most luxurious robe of cloth of gold. Her ladies remonstrated with her. It was not seemly to change on the side of the road neither should her best dress be worn just for the earl's benefit but Margaret would not allow anyone to outshine her, especially not an earl.

The procession was so large by the time it reached York that it couldn't fit through the city gates and an opening had to be made in the city wall to allow more people to filter through. Margaret was escorted to the Minister where she was greeted by the Archbishop of York, the Bishop of Durham, the Abbot of St Mary's and other clergymen. At the altar, she made an offering and gave thanks for her safe journey so far before retiring to the archbishop's palace. The next day she heard Mass in a church so packed out with nobles and common folk 'it would be impossible for them to be numbered'[8] before being feted with a magnificent banquet back at the palace.

Continuing on her journey, the Earl of Northumberland and his entourage accompanied the procession to the delight of all who saw him. Known as 'Percy the Magnificent' he put on quite a show with his displays of horsemanship as they travelled through Northallerton, Darlington, Durham, and on to Newcastle where he had arranged a sumptuous banquet 'which lasted to midnight, for cause of Games, Daunces, Sports and Songs'.[9] Margaret was introduced to Lord Dacre, her father's Warden of the Western Marches, the border lands, at Newcastle. At the time he was yet another new face and yet another person to greet but he would come to feature heavily in the new life she would embrace as Scotland's queen.

On they travelled through Morpeth to Alnwick, where the Earl of Northumberland, lord of such a vast county, had arranged for Margaret to go hunting in his park. She was absolutely delighted to stop and relax for a time. The journey had been a whirlwind of meet and greets with Margaret being on her best behaviour and acting as a new queen. Now she could let her hair down just a little and grabbing her arrows, she 'kylde a Buk with her Bow'.[10]

Back on the road, the end was in sight and they reached England's border with Scotland on 30 July at Berwick, to the resounding sound of cannon fire. Here she paused for two days 'where she had great cheer of the said Captain of Berwick, and her company in like wise. The same day was, by the said captain, to the pleasure of the said queen, given courses of chase within the said town, with other sports of bears and of dogs together'[11] while the final preparations were made for her entry into her new kingdom.

On 1 August, Margaret crossed the border and travelled four miles to the church or kirk at Lamberton. The Earls of Surrey and Northumberland led the way followed by the nobility, officers of arms, her ladies and the rest of her two thousand strong entourage. Margaret chose to ride in her litter wearing a dress of cloth of gold with pearls entwined in her hair for her entrance as James IV's bride and Scotland's new queen. As she made her way to the pavilions assembled for her reception, a triumphal fanfare sounded. The Archbishop of Glasgow welcomed her on behalf of the king surrounded by Scottish nobles, who, determined not to be outdone by the English, wore costly velvets, silks and damask, their arms and crests embroidered onto their jackets. As the nobles knelt in abeyance in front of her, Margaret felt a thrill but now she was safely delivered into the care of the peers of her new realm, it was time for the majority of her English entourage to leave, including the Earl of Northumberland who in typical fashion reared his horse and with a wave galloped into the distance. Margaret knew that many of her people would leave but it made her change in position all the more real.

She was escorted on to Fast Castle for the night. Margaret was shocked at the sight of this imposing castle, a cliff top fortress overlooking the wild North Sea and far removed from the palaces and manor houses she was so used to. However it was safe and secure and she received a heartfelt welcome from Lady Home, the Bishop of Moray's sister while her retinue stayed at the nearby Coldingham Abbey. The next night was spent at a nunnery in Haddington and on 3rd of August Margaret reached Dalkeith Castle, owned by the Earl of Morton, to make ready for her state entrance into Edinburgh and her marriage to the King of Scotland. James was too impatient to wait for her any longer and rode out to meet her causing a flurry of activity at the castle amid cries of 'The king! The king is coming!' Although James had spent a fortune ordering his wedding clothes from Paris, for his first meeting with Margaret he dressed more informally in a crimson jacket with his hawking lure slung over his back as if he had just dropped in after a day's hunting. He dashed into her well-appointed chambers where Margaret dropped into a deep curtsey in front of the man she would share her life with and James gently raised and kissed her before kissing her ladies and welcoming the Earl of Surrey and his wife. Then James took Margaret aside to speak privately. James was pleased with what he saw, even though Margaret was not much older than his eldest daughter. For Margaret's part she couldn't take her eyes off his extremely long beard which she vowed to deal with later. They exchanged pleasantries before a supper was held in their honour and James deferred to his little queen by letting her wash her hands before him and allowing her to take the first choice of food. When the minstrels began to play, Margaret knowing she was the woman of the moment, danced before the king with the Countess of Surrey delighting in his attentions until he returned to Edinburgh.

The evening had gone well until a fire broke out in the stables killing two of Margaret's palfreys. She was distraught at such a terrible end to her stay at Dalkeith and the following day she moved to Newbattle Abbey where James 'flying as the bird seeks her prey'[12] sought her out to offer his sympathy and arrange for entertainments to take place to take her mind off her loss. The king played upon the lute and the clavichord to Margaret's delight and ballads were sung all evening. The next day, the Earl of Surrey presented James with a superb courser, a gift from Henry VII, with green and white damask trappings and two days later, on the 7th of August, James IV presented Margaret with new palfreys resplendent in 'golden harness, velvet saddles and embroidered cloths'.[13]

Margaret was grateful for all the gifts but she was anxious and twitchy. Today was the day she would enter Scotland's capital city of Edinburgh. She began her journey in her litter dressed in a cloth of gold gown adorned with black velvet and ermine trimmings with a collar of pearls and jewels, her new palfreys trotting behind her. About a mile out of Dalkeith she was presented with another gift from the king, a tame deer, for her to enjoy hunting but the Earl of Surrey, wanting their entrance to go smoothly, suggested that any hunting to be done should wait until the king was present.

It wasn't long before James rode out to meet his new queen, dressed in a fine jacket of cloth of gold bordered with purple velvet and black fur. He wore a doublet of violet satin, scarlet hose and his linen shirt was edged with pearls. To add to this magnificent picture, his horse was also draped in cloth of gold and James looked every inch a king. Leaping from his steed, he kissed Margaret soundly and then ordered a horse be brought so that they could ride together. James tried the courser first by getting his groom to sit behind him. When the creature decided to buck and shift, it was felt Margaret would be safer on one of her palfreys, riding pillion behind the king.

In this way they travelled to Edinburgh where just before the city walls a theatrical display was put on for her entertainment.

...whereof came out a knight on horseback, armed at all pieces, having his lady paramour that bare his horn; and by adventure there came another also armed, that came to him and robbed from him his said lady, and at the absenting, blew the said horn, whereby the said knight understood him, and turned after and said to him; 'Wherefore hast thou this done!' He answered him, 'What will you say thereto!' 'I say that I will prove upon thee that thou hast done outrage to me.' The other demanded him if he was armed; he said, 'Yes.' 'Well then,' said the other, 'prove thee a man, and do thy devoir.' In such manner they departed, and went to take their spears, and ran, without striking of the same; after the course they returned with their swords in their hands, and made a very fair tourney; and the caller caused the sword for to fall of the defender: notwithstanding the caller caused to give him again his sword, and began again the said

*tourney, of more fair manner, and they did well their devoir, till that
the king came himself, the queen behind him, crying 'Peace,' and
caused them for to be departed. After this the king called them before
him, and demanded them the cause of their difference. The caller
said: 'Sire, he hath taken from me my lady paramour, whereof I was
in surety of her by faith.' The defender answered: 'Sire, I shall
defend me against him in this case.' Then said the king to the said
defender: 'Bring your friends, and ye shall be appointed a day for to
agree you; whereof they thanked him, and so every man departed
them for to draw toward the said town.*[14]

To end the drama, the deer was let loose and a greyhound set to
chase it through the streets of Edinburgh. But the deer was swift
and found its home back at Holyrood where it was given
protection.

It was time to enter the city through a newly erected wooden
gate with two towers. From the towers, angels sung whilst
Greyfriar monks presented the cross and relics to the king and
Margaret to kiss. The streets were crammed with well-wishers as
the procession made its way through Edinburgh accompanied by
fanfares and minstrels playing. Along the way there were sights
for Margaret to see, a fountain of wine, pageants and mimes. One
depicted Paris 'and the three goddesses, with Mercury, that gave
him the apple of gold for to give to the most fair of the three,
which he gave to Venus'.[15] The city had been cleaned up and
adorned with flowers for her entrance, lending colour to its
austere walls.

Reaching the Church of the Holy Cross, they were greeted by
'the Archbishop of St Andrews, Brother to the said King, his
cross borne before him, accompanied of the Reverend Fathers in
God the Bishop of Aberdeen, Lord Privy Seal of Scotland, the
Bishops of Orkney, Caithness, Ross, Dunblane, and Dunkeld,
and many Abbots, all in their pontifical, with the priests and

canons richly revested, preceded by their Cross'. The Archbishop then gave the king a relic to kiss, but he did as he had done before, deferring to Margaret, and allowing her to go first. After they had made their reverences at the altar it was time to meet the gathered nobles in Holyrood Palace, still under construction, but richly appointed for the coming of the queen. Margaret must have been exhausted but whilst the king was occupied, the Bishop of Moray introduced her around to all the lords and ladies before she could retire to her chamber for a meal and some rest. The eve of her wedding was filled with merriment and dancing with the king until he 'took his leave and bade her good night joyously'.[16]

On the 8th of August 'every Man apoynted hymselse rychly, for the Honor of the noble Maryage'.[17] Margaret shone as the most richly appointed of them all. James had gifted her a wedding dress cut from the same white damask as his own clothes, bordered with crimson velvet. 'Her long fair hair floated loosely over her shoulders; upon her head she wore a rich netted tissue, which hung down to her feet; over this was a golden crown, studded with pearls and other gems, also a gift from the king'.[18] Her ladies dressed in gowns of cloth of gold, crimson and black velvet, satin and tinsel and damasks in many shades.

The time had come. Margaret was escorted to the abbey church between the Archbishop of York and the Earl of Surrey. She wished her father could see her now, dressed in the finest of clothes and looking every inch a Tudor princess and Queen of Scotland. Her retinue took up the left of the church and as the king entered, the Scottish nobles filed in to the right. The Archbishops of York and Glasgow took their place at the altar and James, with his arm around Margaret's waist, led her forward for the ceremony. Afterwards, the Archbishop of York read out a letter from the pope confirming their union. James and Margaret then made silent devotions in front of the high altar where James bid her kneel first 'paying her the most great humility and reverence as possibly might be'.[19] Mass was said and then James placed the sceptre of state into Margaret's hands whilst she was anointed with holy oil and thus confirmed as Scotland's new queen.

The newlyweds now retired to their own chambers for a formal banquet. Margaret's rooms had been recently decorated with tapestries depicting the history of Troy, stained glass windows with Scottish and English coats of arms and the newly created symbol of the rose and the thistle entwined. Under a cloth of gold canopy, she was served course after course seated with just the Archbishop of Glasgow, her ladies and other nobles at their own tables. The first course consisted of a wild boar, brawn and ham, with 12 other dishes served and the second course was of between 40 and 50 dishes – too many to count. Meanwhile James ate with the Earl of Surrey, the Bishop of Durham and the Archbishops of St Andrews and York. When the king was approached by heralds to cry 'largesse' he ordered 'Go ye, cry toward the queen first, that is to wit; Largesse of the high and mighty princess Margaret, by the grace of God Queen of Scotland, and first daughter engendered of the very high and very mighty prince Henry the Seventh, by that same self grace King of England'.[20]

The feasting over both parties joined and 'the minstrels played, and the King and Queen, the Ladies, Knights, Gentlemen and Gentlewomen danced; also some bodies made Games of Pass Pass and did very well'.[21] Margaret must have been thoroughly exhausted and she took time out while the king and many of the gathered nobles attended evensong. Once they were returned, more feasting ensued late into the night. Bonfires blazed across Edinburgh as the people celebrated a marriage they hoped would create lasting peace between Scotland and England.

Yonge, the chronicler, didn't mention any putting to bed or wedding night ritual nor did he see Margaret the next day.

'Touching the Queen, I say nothing for that same Day I saw her not but I understand that she was in good health and merry'.[22] It was a typical custom for the bride not to show herself the day after her wedding. In her absence James attended Mass and dined publicly. An Italian youth played for the king and was sent then to play under Margaret's window so she could still enjoy the entertainment. James's morrowing gift to Margaret was the domains of Kilmarnock. When he visited his new bride in her chambers, her gift to him was the Countess of Surrey wielding shears! As Margaret had vowed to herself, his beard would be cut and in good humour, James submitted even gifting the countess and her daughter Lady Grey 15 ells of cloth of gold and 15 ells of damask respectively for their duties.

Most of Margaret's English retinue that had stayed with her to see her wedded now left for their long journey back to England, although the Earl of Surrey and his wife remained for a time. In Margaret's letter to her father we can see hints of the dislike she felt towards them. She was queen now and fed up of Surrey ordering her household about. She no longer felt like the little girl that she was treated as, she had done her father's bidding and she would now be Queen of Scotland in name and in her actions. She dictated to her secretary:

My most dear lord and father, in the most humble wise that I can think, I recommend me unto your Grace, beseeching you of your daily blessing, and that it will please you to give hardy thanks to all your servants the which by your commandment have given right good attendance on me at this time. And especially to all these ladies and gentlewomen which hath accompanied me hither, and to give credence to this good lady the bearer hereof, for I have showed her more of my mind than I will write at this time.

Sir, I beseech your Grace to be good and gracious lord to Thomas, which was footman to the Queen my mother, whose soul God hath pardon; for he hath been one of my footmen hither with as great diligence and labor to his great charge of his own good and true mind. I am not able to recompense him, except the favour of your Grace.

Sir, as for news I have none to send, but that my lord of Surrey is on great favour with the King here that he cannot forbear the company of him no time of the day. He and the Bishop of Murray ordereth everything as nigh as they can to the King's pleasure. I pray God it may be for my poor heart's ease in time to come. They call not my Chamberlain to them, which I am sure will speak better for my part than any of them that be of that counsel. And if he speak anything for my cause, my lord of Surrey hath such words unto him that he dare speak no further.

But Margaret added in her own hand:

God send me comfort to his pleasure, and that I and mine that be left here with me be well entreated such ways as they have taken. For God's sake, Sir, hold me excused that I write not myself to your Grace, for I have no leisure this time, but with a wish I would I were with your Grace now, and many times more, when I would answer.

As for this that I have written to your Grace, it is very true, but I pray God I may find it well for my welfare hereafter. No more to your Grace at this time, but our Lord have you in his keeping.

Written with the hand of your humble daughter...[23]

It is evident that after all the fuss and pomp of her wedding and her determination to show herself as a true queen, she was now feeling homesick wishing she were back at her father's court. She was still only 13 after all. With most of her retinue gone Margaret's household was mainly Scottish and she struggled to master their accent and understand the unfamiliar words her ladies used. James seemed to be always surrounded by older men who had no time for her. They talked politics constantly and she was too young to take any part in governance nor was she particularly interested in it. The king was either busy with state matters or at his devotions and unlike her grandmother Lady Margaret Beaufort, Margaret was neither pious nor overtly spiritual – she was just bored.

James did his best to make her happy. He created knights for her at splendid ceremonies, put on jousts, arranged hunts, made sure there was nightly entertainments of dancing and music and organised an autumn progress of her dower lands. At least that was something to look forward to. Margaret was determined to take her entire wardrobe with her, packing her belongings into twenty cartloads. Some thought her frivolous and selfish but these things gave her comfort in a world that was suddenly more grim and real than she'd previously experienced.

On the 18th of September, they set out for Linlithgow, James's favourite pleasure palace set on a low hill next to a loch, 17 miles from Edinburgh. In honour of her visit James had had a new south façade built in the English style and floor tiles decorated with their initials placed in his presence chamber. Margaret was delighted with the picturesque palace, it was part of her dower lands, and their stay gave her ample opportunity for relaxing in its sumptuous rooms and hunting in its grounds. These were honeymoon days where they both spent much time in each other's company, dining together and listening to musicians in the evening. James had his court fools, Currie and Daft Ann, entertain them and Margaret for a time could pretend that this is how life should be.

Moving on to Stirling Castle, a defensive fortress perched high on volcanic rock, her happy bubble was burst when she realised James's illegitimate children were housed there. Margaret would have been even further shocked if she had found out that her new husband was still seeing his mistress Janet Kennedy at Darnaway Castle. Margaret was no prude and she knew what happened between men and women, sure she had only just experienced it herself, but she wasn't used to such blatant evidence of it. As far as she knew her mother and father had been faithful to each other and if she had any half-siblings she didn't know of them. To see this brood so warmly greeted by their father was a shock to her and we can only imagine the Tudor tantrum that followed.

With Margaret in a foul temper, they continued their progress North to Falkland, Perth, Scone, Aberdeen and Elgin where they were hosted by bishops and abbots in the local abbeys. Margaret was well looked after and showered with gifts before returning to Stirling. By now James' brood of children had been moved to other accommodation. On the 20th of October they returned back to Linlithgow for three weeks before heading back to the capital for the winter season. Margaret had had to say goodbye to her English minstrels but some Italian musicians were retained for the festivities to come. Her birthday on 29 November was celebrated with magnificence and a day-long round of feasting, dancing, music and a joust. James gave her a *Book of Hours* he'd ordered from Flanders as a wedding gift but it had arrived late. In it were highly decorated pages bordered with butterflies, fruits and flowers and full-page illustrations of the king and queen depicting them at their devotions, a gift to treasure, but it could never replace the book her father had given her.

And she was showered with even more gifts for New Year when James gave her a '"heavy ducat," weighing an ounce of gold...two rings, set with costly sapphires, and on the following day two pearl-studded crosses'.[24] Her ladies were not left out and also received gifts of gold chains and jewellery. Her first New Year in Scotland may have made her homesick but James kept her thoroughly entertained with daily performances of plays and disguisings, music and feasting. Master John, the master of revels and also James' physician and alchemist was charged with organising the performances including a morris dance 'in which six male dancers, attired in dresses of red and white taffety, and one female dancer in a blue robe, all wearing head dresses of blue, red, and variant or various colours, performed sundry evolutions'.[25] For Margaret, the festivities at the Scottish court were as good as at the English and she realised now that Scotland had truly become her home.

Chapter Three

Queen of Scotland
1504–1512

The festivities came to an abrupt end when James IV's younger brother, heir presumptive, also called James and Duke of Ross, died on 13 January 1504 and Alexander, the king's oldest illegitimate son by his mistress Marion Boyd was given his position of Archbishop of St Andrews after his father sought papal dispensation. Alexander was still only a boy of around ten which would mean his father could still receive the revenues of St Andrews until he turned 27, the canonical age for consecration. He was a studious lad, learning Greek, law and rhetoric from the theologian and humanist Erasmus who had met Margaret and Henry as children.

Margaret may have felt his elevation was inappropriate but there was nothing she could do. She was getting used to the favour James showed his illegitimate children. Now the heir presumptive was dead, there was more emphasis on her to produce a legitimate child, something she dreaded and looked forward to equally. She knew it was her duty to deliver the next king of Scotland but she had not long lost her mother to childbirth and the thought of pregnancy scared her. She would not be with child for some time.

In March, Margaret was crowned and presented to Parliament where formal confirmation of her morrowing gift of Kilmarnock was given. Her father appointed Sir Ralph Verney, her chamberlain, Henry Babington, her almoner, and Edward Benstede, her treasurer to act as Margaret's agents in Parliament, and Benstede was immediately given possession of Kilmarnock to keep in her stead.

Margaret was also getting used to James leaving her to travel his country while she preferred to stay at Holyrood, Linlithgow or Stirling. James was a proactive king and he travelled his realm to preside at local courts, dispensing justice and quelling uprisings. Lesley wrote in his *History of Scotland* that 'All theft, rape, murder and robbery ceased in his days by such sharp execution of laws penal, as he caused to be exercised through all the bounds of Scotland'.[1] James even took to disguising himself as a common person so that he could go amongst his people and hear the real state of affairs in his country. His devotions were also extremely important to him and many trips away were spent visiting shrines in self-imposed penance, but in stark contrast he also left Margaret at court while he visited his mistresses.

In the spring, Janet Kennedy, his most recent lover and mother of his son James, Earl of Moray, was taken ill. As she lived close to the shrine of St Duthac he may have used a pilgrimage as an excuse to go and see her. He had sent his doctor, Master Robert Shaw, and freshly produced medicinal potions but finally, overcome with worry, he rushed to her side while she ailed but eventually recovered. In between his trips away James returned to Margaret, after all there was an heir to produce. He was back in April for the Easter festivities at Holyrood when the Lord of Misrule inflicted chaos and merriment on the court to the point of injuring one man so badly the barber was paid by the king to treat his wound. No real damage was intended; it was just high jinks gone awry.

In June a play was put on for their majesties by James Dog, a servant of the court since 1488 who became Margaret's wardrobe keeper. He became the butt of the prolific court poet William Dunbar's satire when Dog refused to give him a doublet that Margaret had gifted him.

When that I shew to him your marks,
He turns to me again and barks,
As he were worrying ane hog;

Madam, ye have a dangerous dog.

When Margaret remonstrated with Dunbar over the incident, he penned another poem that started:

O gracious princess, good and fair,
Do well to James, your wardrober,
Whose faithful, brothermost friend I am.
He is no Dog; he is a lamb.[2]

Dunbar was paid a yearly pension to write for James and 'his professional concern was with the personalities and humours of the court'.[3] Although he received the patronage of the Scottish king, Margaret was particularly pleased with him – when he wasn't deriding her servants – and he reciprocated but penning many verses that spoke of her in glowing colours.

On the 9th of June Margaret and James moved to Linlithgow for nearly a month then went on to Stirling where they heard that Henry VII had sent the next instalment of her dowry plus an extra payment of 5,000 marks for James to cover Margaret's expenses. And she had plenty of them. When she was bored and left to her own devices, Margaret had to find ways to entertain herself and for every new dress she had made, every new jewel she wished to acquire, every musician she wanted to hear, every hunting trip she wanted to take, James footed the bill.

In August, James was off again to quell rebellion along the borders in conjunction with Lord Dacre, Henry VII's Warden of the Western Marches. The border was a notorious trouble spot with 'reivers' raiding and looting inhabitants on both sides. At courts held in Dumfries, Canonbie and Lochmaben James hung many of the rebels and created peace – for a time. He followed up his judicial duties by spending three weeks hawking at Lochmaben before heading back to see the queen at Dunfermline. Margaret left Stirling to meet the king with 35 cartloads of possessions. She had amassed much more since her last trip through James' generosity and gifts freely given. But after just a few days James was off again – this time to the North as far as Aberdeen and Elgin. Margaret waited for his return, despite there being rumours of the plague nearby, and from Stirling they travelled back to Edinburgh for the Christmas season. Margaret dressed to impress that Christmas. Her furrier was so busy lining her gowns an assistant had to be brought in. Or perhaps the queen was suffering with the cold and needed her dresses to give more warmth. Yet again the festivities kept her amused and her life over the next few months became a routine of such pleasures whether she was at Holyrood, Linlithgow or Stirling.

Sometime during the past months, Margaret had been given a more unusual gift – that of two young Moorish girls. Robert Barton was one of three brothers, excellent sailors and captains, with a dash of the privateer to them. They had a long running feud with the Portuguese and the girls had been seized from one of their ships. Years ago, their father had been waylaid on the seas by two Portuguese vessels who captured his ship, the *Juliana*. Complaining to his king, John asked James III to have this theft redressed by Alfonso V, the king of Portugal, but to no avail. James therefore granted John and his sons the right to seize vessels and cargo to the tune of their loss. The two girls came off of one such seizure and were presented to the court. Margaret immediately took them under her wing, naming them Margaret and Ellen. The latter, who came to be known as Black Ellen, became an especial favourite of the queen's and gave her comfort during her husband's absence.

James spent more time away from his wife in 1505 with the advent of a new mistress who was only referred to as 'the L of A' in the treasurer's accounts, a subtle way of noting the many gifts that were showered on the lady. Did Margaret know? After finding out James had so many illegitimate children would this have been any more of a shock to her? We don't know if she ever found out and customarily, she was too busy enjoying the entertainment the king provided for her. On Shrove Tuesday, he had arranged for African musicians to play for his wife including a 'taubronar' or drummer. James was so taken with this drummer that he brought a horse for him so he could accompany him on his excursions and paid to have his drum repainted. At the same event, 12 dancers dressed in black and white costumes performed for the queen. Margaret joined in with such gusto that she began to suffer from nosebleeds. A William Fowler was paid to provide a blood stone, 'a sort of stone supposed to possessed peculiar virtues in staunching bleedings'[4] and also three ounces of undescribed 'stuff' for her treatment.

As the months passed on, Margaret rallied and in May she conceived the king's child. They had precious little time together but in July of 1506 they sailed together from Leith in James' new warship the *Margaret*, named for his queen, to visit the Isle of May, an island in the Firth of Forth estuary. The Isle of May was a popular place for pilgrimages and James urged Margaret to visit the chapel there, dedicated to St Adrian of May, whilst the king visited the pious hermit who lived on its shores. Although their visit was one of devotion the royal couple spent a pleasant evening aboard their ship before one last trip to the chapel and then James escorted Margaret back to Linlithgow.

Henry VII paid the third and final part of Margaret's dowry in August. James's shipbuilding projects were expensive and the money was gratefully received. He had built a new dockyard at Newhaven in 1504 to allow for the building of a bigger ship and commissioned the construction of the *Great Michael* to be built here. In the same month a comet was seen in the sky for ten days. Both Margaret and James hoped it boded well for their future and the child she was carrying. The 17-year-old queen gave birth to their son James at Holyrood on 21 February 1507. He was christened two days later, carried to the chapel on a pillow of cloth of gold trimmed with ermine and proclaimed Prince of Scotland and Lord of the Isles to great rejoicing but for Margaret, everything she had dreaded about childbirth came true. She was desperately ill, weakened by a prolonged labour and if she'd had the strength she would have feared for her life. James certainly did and immediately set out on foot as a pilgrim to St Ninian's shrine at Whithorn, Galloway. The doctors had tried anxiously to revive her strength but James 'would not be soothed by any human consolation...he placed all hope of his wife's recovery in God alone'.[5] It took him seven days to complete the 120 miles and the story says that as soon as he knelt in supplication at the shrine, Margaret miraculously recovered.

A tournament was held in July in Edinburgh in honour of their son and her return to health. Black Ellen, Margaret's gift from Barton, was lady of honour to be protected from challengers by a wild knight, her champion. Dressed in a golden gown trimmed with green and yellow taffeta she made her entrance on a chariot followed by the wild knight and his savages, men dressed in goat skins and antlered helmets. The disguised knight excelled in the joust, defeating all his opponents until with a flourish he removed his helmet so the gathered crowds could see it was the king himself.

James enjoyed the pleasures of court but now his serious side came to the fore. He had urged Margaret to visit St Ninian's shrine as soon as she was able. He was much more pious, wanting to undertake the ultimate pilgrimage and travel to Jerusalem, than Margaret who regularly missed religious services and had to be urged to take up her devotions. The pope had rewarded his piety this year by sending over envoys to present the king with gifts of a purple diadem, wreathed with gold flowers and a 'magnificent sword with a golden hilt and sheath, studded with gems'.[6] He was also given the great honour of being named Protector of the Christian Religion. Now he insisted the queen visited the shrine in person. After the tournament

Margaret agreed to give thanks for her survival, albeit in style. No pilgrimage on foot for the queen but rather by horse and with 17 carts of baggage. It took her a month to travel there and back with leisurely stops in between – more of a progress than an act of faith.

On her return James left again, this time in disguise to 'test the success of his efforts for the suppression of highway robberies throughout his dominions'[7] but they had definitely managed to spend quality time together as by October Margaret was pregnant again. It was her duty she knew but it filled her with fear and absolute dread. She had only just got over the birth of little James. Unfortunately in February 1508, her first born died and it may have helped her to know she was at least carrying another child.

Henry VII had ever been suspicious of Scotland's relationship with France and feared a renewed alliance. When two Scottish nobles, Sir Patrick Hamilton and his brother the Earl of Arran, tried to travel through England on their return home from the French court, the English king had them arrested. Sir Patrick was then allowed to return but the earl was kept hostage. James was furious and Henry quickly sent his ambassador, a young Wolsey, to keep the peace. James kept him waiting at Berwick for nearly a week before allowing him to cross the border. It didn't bode well for his visit and it was the first time that Margaret found herself caught between her husband and her country of birth. She welcomed Wolsey and assured him the king would receive him soon but he was kept waiting for five days more. James 'was so greatly busied in shooting guns and making gunpowder'.[8]

When Wolsey was eventually seen by the king, he stressed that allowing these nobles to travel in England without a safe conduct pass from Henry VII looked suspicious and jeopardised their existing peace treaty. James said he knew nothing about it but wanted the Earl of Arran released. Wolsey countered that this could be arranged but that the earl should swear an oath to return to England if asked. If that was the case, the Scottish king retorted, he would have him hung when he returned to Scotland rather than be an instrument of the English.

Wolsey told Henry VII that no one was ever less welcome in Scotland as himself. The Scottish were pro-French and there was much anti-English feeling. His only allies were Margaret and the Bishop of Moray. Sir Patrick Hamilton had told the queen that her father had treated him well but Wolsey suggested 'he reported opposite to the King'.[9] Margaret tried her best to defend her father but no one was listening. Wolsey likewise was completely frustrated by James and 'encountered such inconsistency that he could not conceive what report he could or should send'[10] back to Henry VII. James finally played the family card saying he would be a good son-in-law if Henry was 'loving, kind and like a good father'.[11] Wolsey returned to England and the Earl of Arran was released.

France still wanted their alliance renewed and Louis XII sent Lord d'Aubigny and Sir Anthony d'Arcy, Sieur de la Bastie, to speak with James about renewing the 'auld alliance'. Wolsey had received the coldest of welcomes but the French ambassadors were well feted and entertained. There was a repeat performance of Black Ellen with her wild knight and late night feasting, dancing and musical entertainments. Unfortunately the trip had been too much for d'Aubigny whose sudden death ended any negotiations. As well as sending condolences to France, Margaret knew that if her father did not hear of the French visit from the king himself it would cause more trouble between them. She asked James to send word and the Bishop of Moray was duly dispatched to give a full report. Henry VII responded by sending James a gift of horses and the Scottish king returned their renewed pleasantries by sending Henry horses from Galloway and superb hunting hawks.

For the moment there was peace between England and

Scotland. It was a huge relief to Margaret, who in July, took to her chambers in Holyrood for the birth of her next child. Petrified by the thoughts of going through another torturous labour, the queen could scarcely contain her anxiety and not only did she suffer again but her baby daughter died soon after. Devastated and unable for court life, James whisked her away to relax at Falkland Palace for the next six months. They didn't return to Edinburgh until January 1509 and then moved on to Stirling for the summer but tragedy wasn't behind Margaret yet and in April she heard of her father's death at Richmond from tuberculosis and his burial next to her mother in Westminster Abbey. His demise had been kept secret for two days as the political wheels of the Tudor court turned until on 24 April heralds were sent into London, announced by the sound of trumpets to declare 'Henry the Eighth, by the Grace of God, King of England and France and Lord of Ireland'.[12]

Now her younger brother, just short of his 18th birthday, would reign and she was quick to send him her congratulations. It had been six years since she had seen him and the once precocious child had turned into a strong-willed young man. On 11 June, Henry VIII married his brother's widow, Catherine of Aragon, and on the 24th Henry and his new wife were crowned together at Westminster Abbey. Margaret knew he would be celebrating in style and she wistfully yearned to attend the banquets, jousts and revelries that would accompany his accession. However they were not to last as their grandmother, the formidable Lady Margaret Beaufort, who had played such a part in their upbringing died on the 29th, the same day as James signed a Treaty of Perpetual Peace with England. Margaret had lost both her father and grandmother and so her relationship with her brother became all the more important to her. She was anxious that there would be peace between Scotland and England and urged James to write to Henry.

Henry VIII for his part wrote frequently to the Scottish king, cementing their new relationship. To one letter, James responded:

After our most hardy recommendation, dearest brother and cousin, We have received your loving letters written with your own hand, where through we understand good and kind heart ye bare to us, of the which we are right glad considering our tenderness of blood. God willing we shall bare the same to you, the which ye shall perceive in deed, if it pleasure you to charge us, as knoweth our Lord who have you in his keeping.[13]

Pleasantries for now but storm clouds would soon gather. Margaret was oblivious to the changes in her brother and had no idea what kingship would do to him. She was pregnant again and James, fearing another terrible childbirth for his wife, went on pilgrimage to St Duthac near Tain in Rosshire. His prayers did some good for although Margaret again did not have the smoothest of labours she rallied quickly after the birth of their son, Arthur, named in memory of her elder brother, in October. But by July their son was dead. Margaret had given birth to three children and all had died. They were overwhelmed with grief and Margaret berated herself for the failure of her children to thrive.

Never the pious one, she now turned to God for help and in the spring of 1511 went on her own pilgrimage to St Duthac's shrine. On route she made a state visit to Aberdeen where her warm welcome was a soothing balm to her recent troubles. As she approached the town she 'was met by a number of the burgesses, four of whom, attired in velvet robes, carried a crimson canopy over her head, and thus attended her to the gate, where, amidst the firing of guns, she was received by a long procession of the inhabitants'.[14] Margaret was escorted through the town that had been freshly tidied and decorated with boughs of holly and birch to see a series of 'moralities'. For her entertainment, scenes from the Bible were enacted as well as a depiction of Robert the Bruce and...

> Then came there four-and-twenty maidens young,
> All clad in green of marvellous beauty,
> With hair detressed as threads of gold did
> With white hats all broidered right bravely,
> Playing on timbrels and singing right sweetly;
> That seemly sort, in order well beseen,
> Did meet the queen, her saluting reverently:
> Be blythe and blissful, burgh of Aberdeen.[15]

The court poet Dunbar captured the visit in his poem about 'Blyth Aberdeane' which also mentions the gift Margaret was given by the town burgesses before being escorted to her lodgings.

> At her coming great was the mirth and joy,
> For at their cross abundantly ran wine;
> Unto her lodging the town did her convey;
> Her for to treat they set their whole ingine.
> A rich present they did to her propine;
> A costly cup that large thing would contain,
> Covered and full of coined gold right fine:
> Be blythe and blissful, burgh of Aberdeen.[16]

While Margaret prayed for an heir to the Scottish throne, the relationship between Scotland and England began to sour. The famous Barton brothers had continued looting Portuguese ships but Sir Andrew Barton, who had been commissioned to protect Scotland at sea, had this time chosen a Portuguese vessel that was carrying English goods in English waters off the Kent coast. Now Henry VIII sent his admirals, the Howard brothers, to intercept him. An anonymous poet captured the fight that ensued:

"Fight on, my men," Sir Andrew said
A little I'm hurt but not yet slain.
"I'll just lie down and bleed a while,
"And then I'll rise and fight again.

"Fight on my men," says Sir Andrew Barton,
"These English dogs they bite so low;
Fight on for Scotland and Saint Andrew
Till you hear my whistle blow!"[17]

But Barton did not rise again. During the battle he was captured and later died of his wounds. When James heard the news, he flew into an almighty rage and accused Henry of breaking their peace treaty. Henry, the fledging king, coolly informed him 'it did not become a prince to levy the breaking of a treaty against another prince for bringing a pirate or thief to justice'.[18] The Howards had taken all of Barton's men to be tried for piracy but Henry had let them go giving them 20 days to leave England. He retorted 'If I had shown justice instead of mercy, Barton's men would have been as dead as Barton himself'.[19] His words only incensed James further.

Thus the Scottish king turned to making sure his ships were seaworthy should they be needed. Henry VIII, unlike James, was no friend to France and across Europe hostilities were brewing. James wanted to be prepared for any battle at sea. His magnificent warship the *Great Michael* was near completion. Measuring 120ft by 36ft, many believed it could never sail. The historian Lindsay wrote that its construction had used 'all the woods in Fife'[20] and more timber had to be found as far away as France and Norway. It carried 'many cannons, six on every side, with three great bassils, two behind on her deck, and one before, with three hundred shot of small artillery — that is to say mijand, and battered falcon, and quarter falcon, slings, pestilent serpents, and double dogs, with baytor and culvering, cors bows and hand bows; she had three hundred mariners to sail her; she had six score gunners to use her artillery, and had one thousand men of warre bye her captains, skippers, and quarter-masters'.[21] Margaret, although fearing the increasing aggression between her husband and her brother, surprised James with a visit on board his ship as he was preparing for its launch. She was three months pregnant and wanted to make the most of her time before her next confinement. They dined on simple fare whilst 'bucks and chickens, fowls and partridges, goats and ox tongues were smoking on the tables at Holyrood Palace, and servants looking in vain for the arrival of their master'.[22]

On 12 October the *Great Michael* was launched, the largest and most heavily armed warship in Europe. It was twice as big as the *Mary Rose*, Henry VIII's warship and knowing that James would have a bigger vessel than he, the King of England ordered the building of the *Henri Grâce à Dieu*. By November, Henry VIII had joined the Holy League against France, organised by Pope Julius II, along with Spain and Venice to counter France's presence in Milan and reclaim papal territories. Needing allies, the French king asked James to renew their auld alliance and Scotland was caught once more between France and England.

Margaret spent the next few months quietly taking time out to visit shrines and chapels to ensure her safety and that of the babe during her next birth. At Christmas in Edinburgh, she didn't take part in the entertainments but watched her servants and guests enjoy themselves before moving on to Linlithgow in March to await the arrival of her next child. But she was still very aware of the political situation. In March, a papal messenger arrived to see James with a declaration against France, hostilities were escalating and the Scottish king tried in vain to sue for peace, writing letters to all the heads of Europe. He urged Margaret to write to King Ferdinand too, using her connection to Spain through her sister-in-law Catherine of Aragon, in a desperate attempt for amity.

European politics now had to be put aside. It was time for her confinement. Luke of the Wardrobe had been paid eight shillings to fetch the 'sark' of St Margaret for the queen and her brother had given permission for the Abbot of Westminster to loan her the relic of the girdle of Our Lady which took pride of place in her bedchamber. On 10 April 1512 a son James was born and baptised the next day on Easter Sunday. He appeared weak at first and they tried three different wet-nurses before he finally began to feed from an Irish woman. Margaret was under no illusions this baby would survive but she prayed all the same. James arranged for an honorary dinner to be given after his son's birth and he sat with his nobles to enjoy 'groaning tables of the good old times'[23] including meat from wild boar, oxen, 'seventeen calves, ninety-four pigs, thirty-five sheep, thirty-six lambs, seventy-eight kids, two hundred and thirty-six birds...'[24] Margaret was unable to attend so soon after the birth but James presented her with a new crimson velvet dress that she could wear once she had recovered.

The English ambassadors, Dacre and West, soon arrived with letters and gifts for Margaret. She organised a reception dinner for them, eager to hear of home, but their visit was not only a celebratory one. Henry VIII had sent his Lancaster Herald over to France with a declaration of war. He was well aware of Scotland's alliance and the ambassadors were charged with 'settling differences'[25] between their own countries to not further antagonise their relationship. As they sat down with James they soon realised the list of grievances on both sides was a long one.

Margaret left them to it but there was one issue that concerned her specifically – her legacy. On her brother Arthur's death, he had bequeathed her his possessions, her grandmother Lady Beaufort had left her jewels and her father also had made provision for her. Her brother had not sent on any of these legacies and James reminded them of that. Dacre wrote to the

Bishop of Durham 'I perceive well that the king taketh great grudge because the queen's duty of legacy is withholden from her; he says it is done in malice of him. No displeasure to the king's (Henry's) grace, meseems it were honourable she were contented therein, considering the sum is so small'.[26] He may have thought it small but Margaret wanted what was due to her and the matter would not rest.

After the ambassadors had returned to England, Margaret took a trip to Whitchurch to pay her devotions before returning to Linlithgow to see her son who was by now thriving. It was a pleasant summer with dinners aboard the *Great Michael*, rowing trips on the loch at Linlithgow with a new boat purchased for her, and feasts and musical entertainments arranged by the king. The threat of war was still in the air but for now, it did not affect her. These were happy months only marred at the end of the year when she gave birth to a daughter prematurely in November. Unlike the growing Prince James, the baby did not survive.

Margaret Tudor

Chapter Four

Flodden and its Aftermath
1513–1514

Margaret presided over the New Year celebrations, giving gifts to her ladies, and joining the court in its festivities, but her previous pregnancy had taken its toll on her and she was severely ill in January and February of 1513. Whether she heard the rumours that her brother Henry was preparing to wage war on France is not certain. These were great times of unrest and the English monarch sent his envoy Dr West to Scotland in March with news. He found Margaret at church where she was giving thanks for her recovery. The Scottish queen was eager to hear of her family and on receiving letters from Henry she commented 'If I were now in my great sickness again, this were enough to make me whole' but she also told West that she 'trusted that Henry had not cast her away'[1] so little had he written to her since his coronation.

When she invited Dr West some days later to dine with her, he informed her that Henry was readying his ships to carry his army to France and Margaret was reported to be 'right heavy'[2] at the news. If England went to war with France, where would that leave Scotland? Henry feared James would take the opportunity while he was away to invade England with soldiers and munitions supplied by the French. West asked Margaret to be instrumental in promoting harmony between their countries and to urge James IV to not do anything to jeopardise the truce they currently held. At this point their conversation was near over, Margaret could only do so much where James was concerned but she had a personal matter to address – where was the legacy, particularly Arthur's, that she still was yet to receive? Henry had craftily told West to use it as a bargaining tool. This, he said, would only be delivered to her if James promised to keep the peace. 'And not else?'[3] was Margaret's reply.

When James heard his wife's legacy was still being withheld he railed at West: 'The Queen shall lose nothing for my sake! I will pay for her myself...'[4] James was in no mood to listen to Henry's blackmail and his request that he write a formal agreement of peace was met with 'you should have no letter of his, nor no new bond to show in France, whereby he might lose the French King'.[5] James was committed to the auld alliance and his agreements with France as West must have known but he pressed the Scottish king for an indication of what actions he might take during Henry's absence from England. Enraged James retorted he didn't care whether Henry was absent or present to which West replied that if he did not give a clear answer as to his planned activities it would be taken negatively. 'You know my mind!' James shouted. West retorted 'he knew neither him nor his mind'.[6] Getting nowhere, the English ambassador left to talk to the Scottish council who agreed with their king and gave no definitive reply. The frustrated West told them 'that if they gave no clearer answer it would be considered as a negative; that they did but trifle with him, and he might waste a twelvemonth in this way'.[7]

The only response he had to send Henry was just a letter from Margaret:

Right excellent, right high and mighty prince, our dearest and best beloved brother,

We commend us unto you in our most hearty wise. Your ambassador, Doctor West, delivered us your loving letter, in which you shew us that where you heard of our sickness you took great heaviness. Dearest brother, we are greatly rejoiced that we see you have respect to our disease, and therefore we give you our hearty thanks, and your writing is to us good comfort. We cannot believe that of your mind, or by your command, we are so fremdly (strangely) dealt with in our father's legacy, whereof we would not have spoken nor written, had not the Doctor now spoken to us of the same in his credence. Our husband knows it is withholden for his sake, and will recompense us so far as the Doctor shews him. We are ashamed therewith, and would God never word had been thereof. It is not worth such estimation as is in your divers letters of the same; and we lack nothing; our husband is ever the longer the better to us, as knows God, who, right high and mighty prince, our dearest and best beloved brother, have you in governance. Given under our signet at our palace of Linlithgow, the xi day of April.[8]

West continued to try and reach a peaceful agreement. He asked for the loan of James' warship the *Great Michael* for England which was turned down. He offered James money as a bribe. He reminded him if he wanted to undertake his planned pilgrimage to Jerusalem he would need England's help but nothing would sway James to any kind of agreement in writing. He still hoped that war could be averted and wrote copious letters to the European heads of state to defer from hostilities. West had to tell him that his non-compliance with England would provoke 'the King to turn his great army upon Scotland'.[9] James answered, 'Yea, my brother shall do right wisely, sith he hath enterprised so great a matter as to make war upon France, which he cannot well perform and bring about, to turn his army upon us, and thereby excuse him of going into France'.[10] West replied, if he broke with England, it might somewhat trouble the King's intended voyage, but would not prevent it. Unbeknownst to James, Henry was already moving troops towards the Scottish border.

West could do no more but before he left he visited Margaret one last time. He saw her there with baby James whom he reported was 'a right fair child, and large of his age'.[11] Margaret gave him gifts to take back to her brother, his wife and her sister Mary. On the other matter she could only say 'I am sorry it is not more favourable'.[12] Not for the first time would she be caught between England's and Scotland's interests. James did write one letter to Henry but it was not what the king wanted to hear. In it James talks of Margaret's legacy who 'for our sake gets not her father's legacy promised in our divers letters. Ye may do to your own as ye think best. She shall have no loss thereof'[13] and made a last attempt to deter Henry from war by asking him to 'supersede his time'[14] and delay his attack. Henry would do no such thing.

On the 30th of July, the king of England sailed for France. Before leaving he made Queen Catherine his regent and left the Earl of Surrey in charge of his troops at home. Henry told Surrey 'I trust not the Scots – I pray you, therefore, be not negligent'.[15] Surrey replied 'I shall do my duty and Your Grace shall find me diligent and to fulfil your will shall be my gladness'.[16] Unhappy at being left in England as an aside Surrey also added, 'Sorry may I see him (James) ere I die, that is the cause of my abiding behind. If ever he and I meet, I shall do all that lies within me to make him as sorry, if I can.'[17] Prophetic words indeed.

As the English king marched his 28,000 strong army towards Thérouanne, James received correspondence from the French king's wife, Queen Anne of Brittany, who appealed to his sense of chivalry by asking for his support. She spoke of him as a knight and she the damsel in need of rescue. With her letters came tokens – a ring, a glove and 14,000 crowns. He answered her call by penning a declaration of war. Before it was sent Margaret tried her hardest to dissuade him, ever wanting to keep the peace. She feared that if her husband challenged her brother it would end in nothing but bloodshed. 'Ye have no reason to assist the French, ye have to keep your promises to England and enjoy peace at home,'[18] she implored him. She scorned Queen Anne and asked James whether her letters would 'prove more powerful with you than the cries of your little son?'[19]

But James could not refuse such an appeal from the Queen of France. James' herald, Lyon King at Arms, was sent to Henry at

Thérouanne to declare war if he would not desist from attacking the French. Henry roared at the poor messenger:

> *Ye have well done your message; nevertheless it becometh ill a Scot to summon a King of England. And tell your master that I mistrust not so the realm of England but he shall have enough to do whensoever he beginneth; and also I trusted not him so well but that I provided for him right well, and that shall he well know. And he to summon me, now being here for my right and inheritance! It would much better agreed with his honour to have summoned me being at home; for he knew well before my coming hither that hither would I come. And now to send me summons! Tell him there shall never Scot cause me to return my face. And where he layeth the French King to be his ally it would much better agreed and become him, being married to the King of England's sister, to recount the King of England his ally. And now, for a conclusion, recommend me to your master and tell him if he be so hardy to invade my realm or cause to enter one foot of my ground I shall make him as weary of his part as ever was man that began any such business. And one thing I ensure him by the faith that I have to the Crown of England and by the word of a King, there shall never King nor Prince make peace with me that ever his part shall be in it. Moreover, fellow, I care for nothing but for misentreating of my sister, that would God she were in England on a condition she cost the Schottes King not a penny.* [20]

There was no way Henry was going to back down. He penned a swift reply accusing James of a 'dishonourable demeanour' and reminding him of the 'righteousness of our cause'.[21] By the time James received it, he was already preparing for war.

Margaret tried everything to prevent her husband from fighting the English. When words were not enough, Margaret told him of her troubled dreams. She had seen him falling from a great height, seen his body bloody and covered in arrows, watched as her jewels turned to tears of pearls. As James dismissed her dreams as mere fancies, Margaret told him 'It is no Dream that ye have but one Son; and him a weakling. If otherways than well happen unto you, what a lamentable day will that be, when ye will leave behind you, to so tender and weak a Successor, under the government of a Woman, for inheritance, a miserable and bloody war'.[22]

By now Margaret may have known that she was pregnant again. It was even more important to her that she not lose her husband in battle. She knew how devout he was and used his piety to try to discourage him. She staged it so that an old man approached the king while at prayer in the church at Linlithgow. He was dressed in blue and white flowing robes and carried a staff much like the depiction of St John in the chapel. His warning was clear; James must not go to war and he was also to 'avoid commerce with women'[23] he said before vanishing 'as (if) he had been a blink of the sun, or a whisp of the whirl wind'.[24] But James was suspicious. Margaret's added touch about adultery made it obvious she was behind the ruse.

When all her ploys failed, Margaret said 'If ye will go, suffer me to accompany you; it may be my Countrymen prove more kind towards me than they will to you; and for my sake yield unto Peace. I hear the Queen my sister will be with the Army in her husband's absence; if we shall meet who knows what God by our means may bring to pass'.[25] James had made his will before heading to join his troops. In it he made Margaret Regent of Scotland should he not return and guardian of their son as long as she stayed a widow plus, along with William Elphinstone, Bishop of Aberdeen, she was to act as his son's tutor thus he felt little James' care was settled. He also made provision for her to receive 18,000 crowns he had accepted from the French King Louis XII to continue the war. James allowed her to accompany him as far as Dunfermline and no further. There they said their goodbyes before Margaret returned to Linlithgow and James IV headed off towards his fate.

The Scottish army crossed the River Tweed on the 22nd of August. Their first task was to besiege Norham Castle which fell after six days. There is a story that when James moved on to Ford Castle he was delayed there by Lady Heron's feminine wiles, giving the English troops more time to take up their positions. If true then Margaret's warning about adultery wasn't heeded. Either way the Earl of Surrey advanced and engaged with James's army on the 9th of September at the Battle of Flodden. Hall, the chronicler, wrote 'the battle was cruel, none spared other, and the King himself fought valiantly'.[26] It lasted just three hours but the devastation it wrecked was untold. Although the English only lost 1,500 men, the Scottish lost around 10,000, many of them the country's leading nobles and their sons. The English took no prisoners and they were triumphant. James IV, King of Scotland, died trying to reach the Earl of Surrey – reports vary as to how he died from arrow to cannon shot. After the battle his body was unrecognisable and would give rise to rumours that he had in fact escaped and finally gone on his pilgrimage to Jerusalem.

Lord Dacre however believed he had found the king's body and had it moved to Berwick Castle to be embalmed and placed in a lead coffin ready for transport to London. A bloody surcoat that James had apparently been wearing made the trip all the quicker and Queen Catherine had it sent to Henry VIII in France as proof of their victory. However, another tale tells us that the body Dacre found did not wear the penitent belt that James always wore next to his skin and that Lord Home, turned traitor, had in fact captured the king, murdered him at his castle and thrown his body in the moat. In the 1750s it would be claimed that a corpse found here complete with iron belt was actually James.

But the body Dacre presumed to be the Scottish king's was duly taken to the monastery at Sheen. Here it would pose a dilemma for Henry on his return. James had been excommunicated by the pope before his death as punishment for breaking the Truce of Perpetual Peace and so was not entitled to burial on consecrated ground. Some reports say that Henry still asked for permission and wished to bury the Scottish king at St Paul's. Instead it seems that it ended up in a store cupboard. Then 'in Queen Elizabeth's time, the supposed body of King James was found by a glazier, who was engaged in repairing the windows. The sweet perfume of the spices induced him to sever the head from the body, and carry it home; after a while, however, he sent it for re-interment to St. Michael's church, Wood-street'.[27] The church consequently burnt down in the Great Fire of London and is now the site of a pub. His head was buried but there is no mention of what happened to his body, presumably it stayed at Sheen. A sad fate for such a king.

All of this of course was in the future. The strange thing was that Margaret never once asked what had happened to her husband's body or request that it be returned to Scotland. From Queen Margaret's Bower, her tower at Linlithgow, she had watched for a messenger to bring her news but she had always known what that news would be. She never expected the king to return and her attention now turned to their son, James, the next king of Scotland. She moved swiftly to Stirling Castle, a much stronger and easily defended position and called the remaining Scottish nobles to her. While she waited for them to attend her, she sent letters to Henry urging him to now be at peace with Scotland for the sake of her son. A melancholy council was held on the 19th of September to approve 'James, by God's grace, King of the Scots, and Margaret, Queen of Scotland, and testamentary tutrix of the same'.[28] And the decision was made:

An it please the queen's grace, that the king our sovereign lord be crowned on Wednesday next to come, the 21st day of this instant month of September, in the kirk of the castle of Stirling, and that my

lord of Glasgow be executor officii, and provide therefor, and that all
other necessary provision be made for the said coronation against
the said day.[29]

The so called 'mourning coronation' was a solemn affair with the ranks of lords so sadly depleted after Flodden. James Beaton, the Archbishop of Glasgow held the crown over the 17-month-old king's head watched by the Regency counsellors Angus, Huntly and Home, the Bishops of Argyll, Orkney, Dunblane, Caithness, Galloway and Aberdeen and the earls of Argyll, Lennox, Eglinton, Glencairn, Atholl, Morton and Crawford. Men who would now assist Margaret in governing Scotland.

The young king established, Margaret had to turn her attentions to the aftermath of Flodden. She had inherited a country of 'despairing widows and fatherless men'[30] and on the 26th of September a proclamation was made to prevent the looting of houses and molesting of women. Women were left without the protection of their men and a second proclamation was necessary to underline that it was treason to deflower or rob maidens and widows on pain of treason. As the country was in turmoil so was the government. Some of Margaret's advisors wanted to negotiate peace with England, others wanted to retaliate. Lord Dacre, on Henry's orders, was still patrolling the borders, asserting English dominance, while Surrey's troops left the area.

Henry VIII had no intention of continuing a costly war, his coffers depleted by his French foray. His queen, Catherine sent Friar Bonaventure Langley to comfort Margaret in her loss and to arrange a truce. Although Catherine's meaning was well, Margaret had no need of succour. Her husband was gone but her child was king. The truce was the most important thing now. Henry responded to her letters. 'If the Scots want peace, they can have it'[31] but it would be the start of a long and troubled relationship between Margaret and her brother. And her Scottish council.

France sent a ship carrying munitions to enable the Scots to continue the war with England. When Margaret met with the council at Perth to discuss Langley's peace overtures she was ignored. Revenge was in the air and it was decided all the Scottish shires should prepare to return hostilities. An envoy was sent to the king of Denmark to ask for help and their relationship with France was also debated. French ambassadors soon arrived with letters from King Louis XII and John Stewart, the Duke of Albany. Albany's father was Alexander, the second son of James II, who had been banished to France for treasonable practices against his brother James III. As such he had been James IV's cousin and had a claim to the Scottish throne. He would reluctantly play a much greater part in Margaret's life but for now, he offered his help in defeating the English. The council were delighted but any help from France was slow to arrive and with Dacre still causing trouble along their borders, a peace truce was agreed for a year and a day in February 1514. Margaret urged the council to send envoys to England to arrange a more permanent solution but to them it just seemed as if she was on Henry's side. They had accepted her regency for now but they would never forget that she was sister to the king who was responsible for the deaths of thousands of Scottish men.

In March 1514, Parliament met at Edinburgh. Margaret, being eight months pregnant, was unable to attend but she sent an opening speech to be read out that thanked its members for their hard work and support of herself and her son. Unfortunately her absence gave its members the opportunity to take control of the chief fortresses in Scotland formerly under Margaret's authority and to further discuss their plans for Scotland. A strong faction was developing in favour of bringing the Duke of Albany to Scotland to govern the realm.

On 30 April, Margaret gave birth to James IV's posthumous son, Alexander, Duke of Ross, at Stirling, named for James' eldest illegitimate son who had died alongside him at Flodden. By the end of May she was well enough to be publicly churched and invited her council to attend a celebration of her son's birth. She could feel the tension and sense that change was occurring. She also heard the rumours that the council wanted to her marry her off to the King of France or perhaps the Emperor Maximilian, even the Duke of Albany who was actually happily married. It was time to assert her influence.

She called a convocation to meet in July at Edinburgh to discuss Scottish policy. Dressing in her best gown, she drew herself to her full height and addressed the nobles with distinction and authority urging them to set aside their differences for the good of the realm. She received the response she wanted. 'Madam, We are content to stand in one mind and will, and to concur with all the lords of the realm, to the pleasure of our master the king's grace, your grace, and for the common weal; and to use none other hands, now nor in times to come, in the contrary thereof.'[32] She had won them over and two days later, when Parliament met they agreed to send messengers to England to sue for a longer peace as Margaret had wished. Content that all was well, Margaret retired to Perth for the summer but it was here in August that she made her biggest mistake.

We don't know when Margaret first met the dashing Archibald Douglas, 6th Earl of Angus but in the autumn she married him in secret at Kinnoull Church. Lindsay of Pitscottie, the Scottish historian, mentions he was on the Scottish council in March 1514 and 'was very lusty in the sight of the Queen'.[33] Both his father and uncle had been killed at Flodden and his title came down to him from his grandfather, 'Bell-the-Cat', after his death the same year. He had been married before to one Margaret Hepburn who died in childbirth and was currently betrothed to Lady Jane Stewart of Traquair, but his maternal grandfather Lord Drummond pushed him to woo Margaret. They were a powerful family and this would be a chance to rise even higher. Knowing that other nobles would be angered by the marriage, a kinsman of Drummond's was called in to officiate at their wedding.

But it was a secret that could not be held for long. When the council members heard the news they were divided in their loyalties. Some had only supported Margaret in deference to their late king. Now she had married, and to a Douglas at that, clan rivalries came to the fore. The Earl of Arran incensed at the match rode for Edinburgh with his men behind him to demand that control of the country be placed in his hands. Some felt that Margaret had violated James IV's will and authority should no longer be hers. The council refused to let Arran take charge but Margaret's marriage was a problem. What had she been thinking to jeopardise her position so? By Scottish law a woman marrying a second time gave up the right to her children and the office of tutrix, but Margaret argued that she was not just any woman but the Queen Regent and her new husband was now co-regent. James IV had named her tutrix in his will but the councillors now argued that she had married beneath her and so forfeited her regency and her rights. Lord Home is reported to have said 'We have shown heretofore our willingness to honor the Queen contrary to the ancient custom of this kingdom; we suffered and obeyed her authority the whiles she herself kept her right by keeping her widowhood. Now she has quit it by marrying, why should we not chuse another to succeed in the place she has voluntarily left? Our old laws do not permit that a woman should govern in the most peaceable times, far less now when such evils do threaten as can scarcely be resisted by the wisest and most sufficient men'.[34]

On the 26th of August Margaret was called before the council. She was told in no uncertain terms that they had agreed that the Duke of Albany should return from France to assume the regency and she was asked to give up her authority. Whilst other meetings continued to discuss her position regarding her son, Sir William Comyn, Lyon King-at-Arms was sent to haul the Earl of

Angus in front of the council for marrying the Queen Regent without their consent. Apparently when he went to deliver the message, the elderly Lord Drummond boxed Comyn's ears for referring to Margaret as my Lady Queen and he was sent on his way without speaking to Angus.

Whilst Margaret struggled to retain her power, plans were afoot to recall Albany. Henry fully supported his sister at this time and urged Margaret to do her best to dissuade others from inviting a new regent to Scotland. With Margaret in charge he had some hope of influencing her but with the duke there, a man who had served the kings of France from the age of twelve, he feared the stronger French alliance that the duke would bring. But the Scottish nobles had made their decision and on the 18th of September Parliament sent a formal request for the duke to come to Scotland 'in all possible haist'.[35] The request was carried by Sir Comyn who was probably only too anxious to escape the growing unrest at home. Yet Albany was not willing to take the regency just yet. He wanted his deceased father Alexander to be cleared of all charges of treason and his family's ancestral rights restored.

Margaret still had a chance to rule but her supporters were waning. Attending a Parliamentary meeting, she realised many were now against her and many more were for Albany. She decamped to Stirling where she called another session in her own right as Queen Regent. However, the council forbade anyone to attend her and she was asked to give up the Great Seal which Angus had wrested from the Lord Chancellor Beaton, Archbishop of Glasgow. Margaret also further antagonised the Scottish nobles by nominating Gavin Douglas (Angus' uncle) for the archbishopric of St Andrews, a position once held by James IV's son, Alexander, who died at Flodden. It had temporarily been held by William Elphinstone, Bishop of Aberdeen, before his death and now three candidates vied for the position. Hepburn was prior there already, and Forman was the man supported by the pope but it was Gavin Douglas, with the help of his clan, who seized St Andrews Castle, the seat of the archbishopric. The council declared that Margaret had no right to appoint him and a siege ensued with Hepburn trying to take the castle back. Margaret had sent Angus to help his uncle and in a long letter to her brother Henry that she wrote from her stronghold at Stirling she asked for his support:

Right high and mighty prince and dearest brother, I commend me to you with all mine heart. I have received your loving and comfortable writings from a man of the lord Dacre's, the 22d day of November, wherein I perceive your fraternal love and kindness. I and my party were in great trouble of mind, till we knew what help you would do to us. I have shewn the said writings to all my lords which were with me in my castle of Stirling the said day, whereof they were greatly comforted. My party-adversary continues in their malice and proceeds in their Parliament, usurping the king's authority, as I and my lords were of no reputation, reputing us as rebels; wherefore I beseech you that you would make haste with your army, both by sea and land, and in especial on the chamberlain, which is post of this conspiration, for within this se'nnight he took an escheat of a bastardry, to the value in ready money of ten thousand pounds, of usual course of Scotland, to his own use, as (though) he had the whole authority. On that other side the prior of Saint Andrew's, with the power of my contrary party, has laid siege to the castle of Saint Andrew's, which I would that your navy would revenge; for it stands on the sea-side fore-against Berwick by north. I have sent my husband to break the siege, if he may, this 23d day. I am at great expenses — every day a thousand in wages, and my money is near hand wasted; if you send not the sooner other succours of men or money, I shall be super-expended, which were to my dishonour: for I can get no answer of my rents, as I shewed you before. All the hope that my party adversary hath is in the duke of Albany's coming, which I beseech you to let in any wise; for if he happen to come before your army, I doubt that some of my party will incline to him for dread. I shall keep this castle with my children till I hear from you. There is some of the lords that dread that your army shall do them scathe, and that their lands shall be destroyed with the fury of the army: wherefore I would that you wrote to them that their lands nor goods shall not be hurt, and, if so be, that they shall be recompensed double and treble. The king, my son, and his brother, prospers well, and are right lifelike children; thanked be Almighty God. It is told me that the Lord's adversaries are purposed to siege me in this castle. I would, therefore, that the chamberlain were holden waking in the mean time with the borderers. I trow that I shall defend me well enough from the others till the coming of the army. I pray you to give credence to master Adam Williamson in other things as it is written to him, and thank him for his good service, and the peril that he was in for my sake in the ship that was broken, with other three ships that I have word since that, departing of Scotland afore his ship, with a message to the duke of Albany, wherein was Lion the herald, with other messages direct from these lords adversaries, with letters sealed with the great seal, which seal they keep masterfully from me and my lords, and use it as they were kings. I trust that God is on my party, which letted their message, and furthered mine. I have given Saint Andrew's to the apostolate of Arbroath, my husband's uncle, wherefore I would that you letted all other competitors that labour the contrary in Rome, and that you would direct to the pope's holiness upon the same with the next that you send, and that you would direct writings to me each month, at the least, how you will do, and what you would that I did ; and if my party-adversary counterfeit any letters in my name, or if they compel me to write to you for concord, the subscription shall be but thus — Margaret R. and no more, and trust that such writing is not my will. Brother, all the welfare of me and my children lies in your hands, which I pray Jesus to help and keep eternally to his pleasure.

At Stirling, the 23d day of November.

Your loving sister, Margaret R.[36]

Margaret knew there were spies everywhere and her position was precarious. This letter was not intercepted and it set up the use of her signature as proof of whether she had written the letter to Henry or not. If further correspondence was sent 'from your loving sister, Margaret R' it had come from her hand, if it was only signed 'Margaret R' it was false or she had been made to sign it.

Henry had promised troops and Margaret now asked that they be sent but they would not arrive. Henry had changed his mind fearing he would upset the delicate peace England had found with France. Margaret's sister Mary had married King Louis XII in October but the marriage had been short-lived. Louis died on 1 January 1515 and Henry had to both protect his younger sister and make an alliance with the new king, Francis. Margaret would have to wait.

Chapter Five

A New Regency
1515–1516

Instead of sending his army, Henry VIII suggested that Margaret escape to England with her sons. For now her eldest, James V, was the English king's potential heir – Henry's wife Catherine had had four children since their marriage but all were either stillborn or died shortly after birth. Henry proposed that Margaret's eldest son become James of England whilst her younger son Alexander have Scotland. Throughout the aftermath of Flodden, Margaret had clung to one thing and that was that her son was the true king of Scotland and she would do all in her power to see him rule. Without upsetting her brother, she had to put him off and so wrote:

> *Yet it comforts mine heart to hear your fraternal desire; but it is impossible to be performed by any manner of fashion that I, my husband, or his uncle can devise; considering what watch and spies there is daily where I am, and I dare disclose my counsel to none other but God. If I were such a woman that might go with my bairn in mine arm, I trow I should not be long from you, whose presence I desire most of any man.*[1]

But Henry would not be put off. All his correspondence now went through Lord Dacre at Berwick. Margaret sent two of her men, Williamson and Inglis, to explain her situation but Williamson felt she should heed her brother and wrote:

> *Madam, I beseech your grace, at the reverence of God, for your own singular weal, and for the promotion of [your] children, my native king and prince, to follow the advice and counsel of your dearest*

brother the King of England, which intendeth only for your weal and the promotion of your sons. Your enemies labour to make peace with your brother the king. I have seen their writings since Sir James departed from me. What inconveniences may fall to your hurt thereof, your grace may soon understand. Prevent your enemies, _and do after your brother's counsel; and if ye so do, I ensure you, madam, by great possibility, your sons shall be the greatest Scotchmen that ever was.[2]

Margaret felt that if she ever left Scotland with her sons it would be to give up James V's right to the throne and that she could not counter. She explained on another occasion why she could not come:

My lords hath ordained a Parliament to be holden at Perth the 12th day of March, and to warn all the lords of Scotland to be there, and they that refuseth to come to be reputed as rebels.[3]

If she was labelled a rebel, her son would have no chance. Parliament met but no decisions were made. Dacre wrote at the time 'There was never so much disorder in Scotland as there is now – pray God it continue'[4] – Henry's man to the last. The Sottish council were waiting for Albany to arrive and Henry was doing his best to keep him in France. Through Margaret, Henry still held some power but with a new regent, his control would slip. He sent his right-hand man Charles Brandon to negotiate with Louis XII's successor, King Francis, mainly on the widowed Mary Tudor's behalf, but also to urge the king to delay sending Albany to Scotland saying that the duke 'is the most suspect person that might be sent, for the surety of the two young princes, because he aims at the crown of Scotland'.[5] But Brandon told Henry he had met with Albany who assured him 'that he trusted that his going should do good, for he entended to reduce them of Scotland to be contented to take such a Peace'[6] and Mary had also asked the duke to protect her sister and her sons.

King Francis had given the duke permission to sail for Scotland, he could not delay him any longer and in April, Albany was on his way. The English ambassador Wingfield confirmed Henry's fears 'he shall keep his voyage, in so much as he departed yesterday towards Orleans and from thence to St Malo. I pray God that the said unhappy Duke be not occasion of too great evil and inconvenience'.[7] The Duke of Albany's ships were spotted off the coast on 17 May 1515 and the next day he landed at Dumbarton, evading Henry's ships that were sent to deter him. With him came eight ships, full of provisions and 1,000 French soldiers. Lord Home, Margaret's enemy until now, greeted him with a huge entourage of 10,000 horsemen on the quayside. Albany, who spoke very little English, made a condescending quip in Latin which infuriated Home and instantly made an enemy of him. He was insulted enough to now turn his allegiance to Margaret who had been anxiously awaiting the duke's arrival. To start their relationship off on the right foot, she vacated her apartments at Holyrood Palace for his use and took up residence in Edinburgh Castle. For their first meeting, she dressed in rich red velvet and looked every inch a queen. She spoke to him in French, needing no interpreter, welcoming him to Scotland and hoping he would enjoy his stay. Secretly she hoped it would be a very brief one.

Her first impressions of a genial man, someone she could work with to secure her son's future, was shattered when she was called to a council meeting. The siege of St Andrews Castle had ended when Hepburn took the castle back and Forman, the pope's choice for the archbishopric, then usurped him. To make up for it Gavin Douglas had been given the bishopric of Dunkeld in January. Margaret and Henry VIII had lobbied the pope for his agreement which he gave in February. Gavin was charged of obtaining his position through the English and not by nomination from Scotland and was imprisoned in St Andrews

Castle. Lord Drummond was also imprisoned for striking Lyon King-at-Arms and was imprisoned at Blackness castle even though Margaret spoke up for them both. It was her first clash with Albany.

The duke may have upset Margaret but he made an impression on the Scottish nobles when he held a memorial service for James IV at St Giles Church mid-July 1515, although it isn't certain whether Margaret attended. Albany and his council, dressed in full mourning clothes, entered the church, which was decorated with 140 painted banners, to hear a requiem Mass in the late king's honour. It was rumoured that a servant of Lord Home's told him that James's body was actually at Home Castle but he refused to be drawn in.

On the 12th of July Albany opened Parliament where his regency was confirmed. He was ceremoniously handed the regal sceptre and sword of state by the Earl of Arran. In a move that must have galled Margaret her husband and the Earl of Argyll then placed a coronet on Albany's head. Business that day included the pardoning of Lord Drummond, although his estates were forfeit to the crown, and more importantly for Margaret, the care of her children. Albany's first task was to ensure the safety of the little king. With the council, he appointed eight nobles as guardians from which Margaret could choose four to look after her sons. Margaret had taken the children to Stirling. She was six months pregnant with Angus's child and refused to relinquish them. She had been told tales of Edward IV's sons since she was young – those princes in the tower who had vanished presumed dead. She did not want her sons to mysteriously disappear too so when a delegation from the council was sent to Stirling to inform her of their decision, she stood firm. Dacre reported her reaction:

And when as she heard tell of their coming, she took the young king in her hand, and the nurse having the prince, his brother, in her arm, within the iron gates, then being open; and with the queen being the

Earl of Angus, her husband, and their servants, but a few number. And when as she saw the lords within three yards of the gates, she bade them stand, and demanded the cause of their coming, and what was their message. And then they showed they came from the duke and governor, and that it was decreed by the Parliament that they should come to ask deliverance of the king and his brother. And then she caused the portcullis be letten down, and made answer, saying that the castle was her own feoffment, given to her by the king her late husband, with other parcels; and that her said late husband had made her protectrix, and given her authority to have the keeping and governance of her said children, wherefore she could in no wise deliver them to any person. Natheless, she desired respite of six days to give her farther answer. And then the Earl of Angus said, and showed openly it was his will and mind that the king and his brother should be delivered, according to the decree of Parliament, and thereupon desired to have an instrument raised, for fear of losing his life and lands.[8]

After the six days had passed, with no help from either her husband or her brother forthcoming, she sent the council a declaration that she wished to remain in the position of tutrix to her children as per James IV's will but that she would allow four guardians – the Earl of Angus, the chamberlain Lord Home, the Earl Marshal Lord Keith, and Sir Robert Lauder, Laird of Basse – to also care for him. Lord Home, however, was currently on the run, after failing to arrest George Douglas, Angus' brother, as ordered by the duke.

Home and Angus, with Dacre's help, planned to rescue Margaret and smuggle her sons across the border but they were thwarted by the Earl of Bothwell and his 500 men who had arrived at the castle. Angus found a way in through an underground tunnel to talk with Margaret but as he was leaving he was attacked and 16 of his men were killed. The Earl then fled back to his estates. Albany had ordered him to assist at Stirling and his desertion was noted. The Duke now arrived with 7,000 armed men. As regent he was to act on James V's behalf, with no James he would not be able to maintain his regency. It was paramount that the young king-to-be and his brother be in his care.

Margaret had few men with her inside the castle compared to the troops that were amassing at her gate. She had no choice but to surrender but she made sure that this was done with full recognition that her son was to rule. She dressed the three-year-old James V in his finest clothes and placed a golden crown atop his head then she led him outside and passing him the heavy keys to the gate urged him to present them to Albany who knelt before the young king. Margaret took the opportunity to ask the duke to look favourably upon her and her husband and to allow her to continue seeing her boys. Albany swore his loyalty to her and her children but Angus was another matter. He would offer no such assurances for a traitor. Margaret was escorted back to Edinburgh whilst the Earl of Bothwell, Lord Fleming, Lord Keith and 140 men were left at Stirling to secure the castle and its precious inhabitants.

Henry VIII was furious. The boys being under Albany's control rather than his own was his worst nightmare. He felt that Margaret had given in too easily. She had accepted the duke's governance without a fight. But Margaret had been willing to fight and Henry had not sent her any support. Now her best tactic was to seem at peace with the duke which still gave her access to her children while trying to placate her brother. Albany had made her sign a formal confirmation that she gave her sons into his keeping. He also asked her to write to Henry to tell him she was content with this arrangement. If Henry had been paying attention he would have seen that she signed the letter with just 'Margaret R' – the signal that all was not well.

Margaret wrote again to Henry from Edinburgh on the 20th of August:

Right excellent, right high, and mighty prince and dearest brother,
I commend me unto you with all my heart. I have received your
writing from Unicorn herald, wherein you reproved me of certain
things that I have done which is not to your pleasure. Verily,
brother, I wrote to you as I found cause, and trust that I and my
cousin the duke of Albany, governor, shall continue on that fashion,
that unity and peace may persevere betwixt both the realms. It is
ordained in this realm, with consent of the governor, in plane (full)
Parliament, that three lords which were most convenient therefor
should have the charge and keeping of the king and his brother, my
sons; which lords I consented to receive. Nevertheless I have
presence of my children at my pleasure, and enter to them whenever
I will. Brother, I am determined that I and my said cousin shall take
one part, for I know it is most for my profit. There ore I pray you
send some wise man to see and know the state, and to make a sure
way betwixt me and him, and write your letters to him thereupon to
entreat me and my children honestly; for I know that he will do the
better to me for your sake. And if I find otherwise, I shall advertise
you by the said wise man that you shall send. My cousin, the king
of France, has sent me writing by this bearer, and prays me that I
will entreat and do my diligence to keep the peace betwixt the
realms, the which I pray you to do in likewise for my re quest.
Brother, I purpose, by the grace of God, to take my chamber and lie
in my palace of Linlithgow within this twelve days, for I have not
past eight weeks to my time ; at the which I pray Jesu to send me
good speed and happy deliverance, and to have you, dear brother,
eternally in his keeping.[9]

This time the letter was signed the same way but it carried the
key information that she would be taking to her chamber at
Linlithgow to give birth to the child she was carrying. Albany
had given her permission and so this letter was allowed to find
its way to her brother. Henry had ordered Dacre to continue to
carry out raids along the border and to employ Lord Home to

carry them out diverting Albany's attention from Margaret's movements. Although she had come to some understanding with Albany, Margaret felt that the only way to win England's support was to head south to her brother and plead with him for men, munitions and money to take control of Scotland once more. On the 1st of September Dacre managed to get a secret message to her. Instead of Linlithgow she should ride for the castle at Blackadder where he would meet her and escort her across the border and into England. Margaret sent her trusty servant Robin Carr agreeing to the plan.

To keep up appearances however she first moved to Linlithgow where Angus joined her. Two days later, in the dead of night, they rode hard for Tantallon Castle, a Douglas stronghold and the following day moved on to Blackadder. Margaret was eight months pregnant and it must have been hard going for her. While they rested at Blackadder however they received messages from Albany asking her to return and if she did they could work out a compromise regarding the children and payment of her dower rents. Up until now they had been withheld and Margaret was in dire financial straits. She was almost swayed by his words. They had eventually come to an understanding and she knew that she might be able to persuade him further and negotiate terms but Dacre, fearing his and Henry's plans would go awry, untruthfully told Margaret that Albany was amassing troops to lay siege to the castle. They rode again for Berwick Castle but the governor there had had no instructions to allow her entry and so they took refuge in Coldstream Priory.

Margaret then contacted Albany. It was her last chance to resolve the situation before she crossed the border. She feared leaving her sons behind and what her removal to England would mean for them. Anxious to come to an arrangement, Albany sent Du Plains, the French ambassador to treat with her but when he arrived he found that she had gone. Wily Dacre hearing they may be reconciled had sent for urgent permission for Margaret to cross into English territory and hearing the ambassador was on his way moved her onwards towards Morpeth Castle, his own residence. Angus had to remain in Scotland for the permission did not allow any Scotsman to cross the border. Margaret couldn't make the 20 mile ride. Two weeks before her time, she felt her labour pains starting. Dacre quickly rerouted them to Harbottle Castle.

Henry and Catherine had sent on the essentials for Margaret's confinement, bed hangings and baby clothes, but they had all been delivered to Morpeth. Harbottle was not prepared for a royal visit nor for a royal birth. This baby was coming two weeks early and Margaret dreaded another prolonged labour and childbed sickness. On 7 October, she gave birth to a daughter, Margaret Douglas, who was baptised 'with such convenience as could or might be had in this barren and wild district'.[10] She was again unwell but this time with searing sciatica that caused her to scream in pain every time she tried to move. With bed rest prescribed, Dacre took over. A letter was sent to Albany from Harbottle seemingly from Margaret but it was Dacre who wielded the pen:

Cousin, I heartily commend me unto you, and where I have been enforced for fear and danger of my life, many things considered, to depart forth of the realm of Scotland into this the realm of England. So it is, that by the grace of Almighty God I am now delivered, and have a Christian soul, being a young lady, desiring you in God's name, and for your honour, as right and good justice requireth, that you suffer me, as tutrix of the young king and prince, my tender children, to have the whole rule and governance, as well of them as of the said realm of Scotland, according to the last will and testament of my late spouse and husband, the late king of Scotland — whom Christ for his passion pardon — approved and confirmed by the pope's holiness, according as his said holiness signifieth unto you and exhorteth you to do, as now I move and require you, and that it may like you to ascertain me how you be minded to do in that behalf, &c.[11]

Albany wrote a terse reply in which he told Margaret 'we cannot consent that you have the tutory of the king's grace and his brother, nor the governance of the realm'.[12] There was not to be an easy solution to her situation. Letters were sent from Margaret to the pope, the king of France and the Venetian ambassadors, making her plight a European affair but none would come to her aid. Her only hope was in her brother who was also writing his own letters telling Francis 'beware, lest the affairs of Scotland injure our friendship'.[13]

At the end of November, Margaret was well enough to be moved, albeit in a litter, to Cartington for a few days then on to Brinkburn priory and finally to Morpeth. It was a torturous journey for her. Sir Christopher Garneys had been sent by Henry to keep him informed of Margaret's progress. He told his sovereign 'I think her one of the lowest brought ladies, with her great pain of sickness...it would pity any man's heart to hear the shrieks and cries her grace giveth, when she is moved or turned'.[14] But Margaret also found pleasure in the gifts that Henry and Catherine had sent to her including 22 dresses and yards of cloth. She was carried into the great hall to be presented with her presents and was joined by her husband and Lord Home to whom she said 'Lo, my lord, here you may see that the king my brother hath not forgotten me, and that he would not I should die for lack of clothes'.[15]

It was a moment's respite from the pain she was experiencing. Dacre became increasingly worried about her, not just because of her health but for safety reasons he wanted her moved down to London, away from the borders and into her brother's care. He asked the king in January 1516 to send another doctor 'trusting much the better, by their good comfort and counsel, to have the sooner recovery of her great infirmity and sickness'.[16] Dacre assured the king there was no danger to her life but the sooner she was better, she could travel. She was so ill they feared to tell her the most devastating news. Back in December her youngest son Alexander had died and they worried she would relapse if she were told. Dacre reported 'I think verily that her grace would take his death unto her great heaviness…in anywise it shall be kept from her knowledge as long as we may'.[17] Margaret would not find out until March.

In the meantime a temporary truce had been agreed between England and Scotland. The Scottish couldn't understand why Margaret would take her troubles to her brother 'to league herself…with England, against the independence of that country of which her son was sovereign, whilst Albany, with much earnestness and sincerety, offered a complete restoration to all those rights and revenues, as queen-dowager, which she has not forfeited by her marriage, was an excess of blindness and perti-nacity difficult to be understood'.[18] But it was exactly those rights forfeit by her marriage that she fought for.

Margaret had not had an entirely poor relationship with Albany and she felt that they may still come to some agreement but she was being manipulated by Dacre. He caught her at a most vulnerable time. Not only was she hurting from losing her youngest son and feeling bereft from being apart from her eldest, but to top it all Angus had visited less and less. He had come to terms with Albany and was back in Scotland and back in the arms of his once betrothed Lady Jane Stewart of Traquair although Margaret was yet to find out this piece of information. The marriage that had cost her the regency and access to her sons was a shambles.

The current truce stipulated that Scottish envoys would visit Henry's court to discuss the situation further. To that end, Dacre took charge of all Margaret's correspondence with Albany and began to compile a book of complaints. The first eight pages concerned Margaret's grievances to which she signed her name. She had listed every slight, from taking her children from her to imprisoning her friends to keeping her poor and suggested that all his actions had forced her to flee Scotland and not only that but she had delivered a baby 'fourteen days before her time, and fell into such extreme sickness that her life was despaired of by all'.[19] The rest was a list of the breaches of law supposedly committed by the Scots since Albany's arrival. Dacre advised Henry that he had finished the book and that Margaret should travel south as soon as possible – to not give her further chance to treat with Albany.

Margaret began her journey on 8 April. She was both excited at her forthcoming visit to her brother's court and anxious that she was leaving her son, the King of Scotland, far behind. Her first stop was at Newcastle, then on to Durham and before York, she was met by the gallant Earl of Northumberland. Margaret couldn't help but reminisce on the time they had last met when she was but a child travelling to Scotland for her wedding. The once athletic Earl had aged considerably, was suffering from rheumatism and was no longer able to put on a show of horse-manship as he had once done. It saddened Margaret to see him and to realise that she too had grown older. She felt it keenly even though she was still only 25.

From Stony Stratford, Buckinghamshire, Margaret wrote to her brother, her spirits lifting as she grew closer to London. 'Dearest brother, as heartily as I can I recommend me unto you, and let you know that yesternight I came hither, so being comforted of you in my journey in many and sundry wises that, loving be to our Lord God, I am in right good health, and as joyous of my said journey toward you as any woman many be in coming to her brother, as I have great cause, and to have sight of your person, in whom next God, is mine only trust and confidence…'[20]

In May, she moved on to Enfield for one night to the home of

Sir Thomas Lovell, Lord Treasurer, and then on to Tottenham where Henry was waiting for her at William Compton's house. For their first meeting in 13 years, Margaret dressed in a purple velvet dress made from the cloth Henry had sent her trimmed with cloth of gold. Henry likewise had dressed finely in green and yellow velvet with a flat velvet cap adorning his auburn hair. Margaret was amazed at how tall and athletic her younger brother had grown but they had no time for reminiscing yet. An escort was awaiting to accompany her into London and Queen Catherine had sent a white palfrey for her to ride to Baynard's Castle where apartments had been made ready for her. After her long journey Margaret was grateful for the comfort of sumptuously appointed rooms filled with beautiful tapestries and exquisite furniture.

Scottish ambassadors had also made the journey to London far quicker than Margaret but were kept waiting. Henry would not speak to them until he had had the full story from his sister. But first there were celebrations to honour Margaret's arrival. She journeyed down to Greenwich where she was reunited with her sister Mary who had returned home after her brief marriage to King Louis of France and was waiting for her with Queen Catherine. All three had recently had children and they had many stories to share and much to discuss. It was a welcome interlude for Margaret to be back in the bosom of her family and to enjoy the delights of the Tudor court. Henry ordered a two-day joust to be held for his sister. Margaret took her place on the dais with Catherine and Mary to watch the tournament unfold. She must have felt a pang for Angus, her missing husband, as the queen cheered on Henry and Mary made much of her new husband, Charles Brandon, Duke of Suffolk. Henry too noted the earl's absence as 'Done like a Scot'.[21] He had given him his permission to accompany Margaret to his court but her husband dared not leave his estates in Scotland for fear of offending Albany and more importantly he wanted to build his powerbase for his future plans.

Margaret had not even heard from her husband as she watched the stars of the joust challenge their opponents. Hall reported that on the first day 'every man did well, but the King did his best'[22] showing off in front of his elder sister no doubt. On the second day, the joust ended when Henry and Charles gave a display of horsemanship running 'volant at all comers'.[23] The celebrations were followed by a banquet in Queen Catherine's rooms where Margaret held pride of place. Before long it was time for an interview with her brother regarding Scotland and her treatment there. Henry urged her to agree that the only way forward was for Albany to give up the regency and return to France. When Henry met with the Scottish ambassadors he told them us much, discussed Margaret's long list of grievances and sent them off with letters to the duke demanding he leave. Albany was actually longing to return to France and his wife, Anne de La Tour, Countess of Auvergne, and suggested he travel through England on his homeward journey. Henry gave his consent eager to have the duke where he could keep him under house arrest or place him in the Tower. But Albany was persuaded to stay by the Scottish council and Henry's plan came to nought.

Negotiations between England and Scotland continued throughout Margaret's stay and her move from Baynard's Castle to Scotland Yard. At one point they heard news that James V was ill and Henry's rage knew no bounds. Again he wrote to Albany to tell him that if the young king died he would be held fully responsible. Margaret feared for her child until she heard that he was in fact recovered from his illness. Her husband too had been pardoned and as much as she wanted to see Angus there was no sign of him joining her.

Some headway was made with the Scottish council who agreed to send on her jewellery, clothes and furniture that had been left behind at Tantallon and other royal residences. She had been solely dependent on Henry for everything – he was even paying her servants – and it was also agreed to help her retrieve the rents from her dower lands. However in her absence many others had taken her money – Angus included although he said otherwise – and the sum of £14,334 she was expecting came to her as a mere £114.

It was with a sense of shame and embarrassment then that Margaret approached the now Cardinal Wolsey before Christmas 1516. She had no money to buy New Year's gifts for her family and it was a matter of pride that she presented her brother and wife with splendid presents in thanks for their hospitality. She asked Wolsey for a loan of £200 and added 'I beseech you heartily that I may have it tomorrow night at the farthest for else I will be disappointed'.[24] Wolsey did not disappoint her.

Craigmillar Castle

Chapter Six

Return to Scotland
1517

Although Margaret was having to beg for money, Henry spared no expense on Christmas festivities. His was a court of wealth and luxury and he was determined that everyone would revel in his extravagance. Meal after meal was served at the Twelfth Night banquet, followed by the wheeling out of a delightful pageant called the Garden of Esperance 'set with flowers...of silk and gold, the leaves cut of green satin...in the midst of this garden, was a pillar of antique work, all gold set with pearl and stone' with an arch 'crowned with gold; within stood a bush of roses red and white, all of silk and gold'.[1] Six lords and ladies walked within the garden and descended from the setting to encourage the court to dance. Margaret was in no mood to join in. She was beginning to feel like she had outstayed her welcome and she was sorely missing her son.

As a new truce between England and Scotland was being discussed, Margaret began to make plans to return. Albany informed her that she would be 'heartily welcome'[2] but that she could only return with 24 English servants, fearing that larger numbers could constitute an army and a bid from Henry to take back the regency by force. Henry and Margaret had continually asked the Scottish council to reinstate Margaret as regent and tutrix but as the negotiations wore on this was a definite point on which the Scots would not back down. She was the little king's mother and she would be welcomed back in Scotland as such but she would not be given back the reins of authority.

On 17 April, she received formal permission from her son to return 'we...with the advice and counsel of our cousin, tutor and governor, John Duke of Albany...have granted...that it be lawful to our dearest mother to come into this our realm, freely and peaceably with her train'.[3] But she still worried that she would be kept away from James. He had been moved from Stirling to Edinburgh and was closely guarded. No one was allowed near him without permission from the governor of Edinburgh castle, Sir Patrick Crichton. That was a battle for another day and first, Margaret had to undertake her journey north. She said her goodbyes to Henry and Catherine at Windsor but not before she had an earnest conversation with her brother. She asked him to allow her to act as mediator between Scotland and England and to take her advice on all Scottish matters. Specifically she wanted no renewals of peace treaties 'unless she were well and honourably treated'.[4] Henry agreed.

By 16 May, Margaret was ready to leave. Henry had gifted her horses with trappings of 'white damask cloth of gold, crimson cloth of gold and black velvet'[5] provided similar cloth for her attendants livery and showered her with jewels, plate and two fine gold cups, and arranged her escort. She was welcomed in each town she stopped at but was unwell at Doncaster. By June she was at York where she received the heartening but unexpected news that Albany was after all leaving Scotland for France. Albany had appointed a council of regency to act in his stead whilst he was away – the archbishops of St Andrews and Glasgow, the earls of Angus, Arran, Huntley, Argyle and his friend and deputy Sieur de la Bastie.

She wrote to Henry:

In my most humble wise I can I recommend me to your grace. Pleaseth you to wit that upon Tuesday Canter came to me to York from the duke of Albany, with writings which I send to your grace, the very copy word by word, because I keep his letter myself; and he hath sent writings to your grace to shew you of his departing out of Scotland, and that the council of Scotland would not suffer him to pass through England, as your grace will perceive by his writings:

howbeit methinks he has taken this purpose very hastily, for I know well he thought it not within this short while. But I may thank your grace and no other, or else it had not been; beseeching your grace as humbly as I can, now, since he doth depart, to look well upon it for my surety and that he may not come to trouble me after, as my special trust is in your grace, for he proposeth to come again into Scotland. Sir, I am sure the duke hath written to your grace how he hath ordered everything now at his departing, and what persons shall have the rule, both the wardens of the borders and within the realm, or else I would have written all at length: for he hath sent me word of everything, and how I shall be received into Scotland, and how I shall be answered of my conjunct feofment, as is made between your grace and him, with the council of Scotland; howbeit I will be plain to your grace, an you will not be displeased, for I say it not for no displeasure to your council, for I think they know not that I know in this matter. Sir, your grace knoweth it is concluded between your council and Scotland that I shall have all that I have right to pertaining to me, with one clause in it, that is, I giving again it that I have pertaining to my son, not declaring plainly what it is; which may be hurt to me in time coming, for the king my husband, whose soul God pardon, ere he went to the field, gave me a letter of his hand, commanding to deliver me 18,000 crowns of weight, that the French king did send; which was without the council of Scotland's consent. And also they may claim any other things that I have that the king my husband gave me, which were wrong. And I spent the most part of it ere I came to your grace, for I was not answered of my living since the field, to hold my house with. And, therefore, I beseech your grace to command my lord Dacres to see a sure way for me and master Magnus, ere I go in. But now the duke goeth away, I set not much by the remnant that is behind: for I know them and their conditions; with fear that they have of your grace they will be glad to please me. I desire this to be done in adventure that the duke come again, that I be not troubled with him. I would not shew this to none but to your grace, beseeching your grace to continue good and kind brother to me, as you have been ever, and that I may hear from your grace; which will be to my great comfort, as God knoweth, whom preserve you. Written at York the 3d day of June. Your humble sister, Margaret.[6]

It gave Margaret hope for the future but at the border she hesitated steeling herself to her return whilst she discussed her situation with Dacre at Berwick. Her husband Angus met her at Lamberton, and Dacre – much more aware of Angus's recent movements than she was, and knowing that he had been ordered to attend his wife – had him sign a memorial 'by which he renounced all manner of right to interfere with the dower-lands, profits, or jewels of the queen'.[7] Other nobles attended including Sieur de la Bastie who welcomed her back to Scotland on behalf of the council and with an escort of 3,000 men accompanied her back to Edinburgh.

Margaret was anxious to see the son she had left for so long and her first concern was to make sure he had been well looked after. She hurried to David's Tower, followed by attendants carrying gifts from England, but was refused entry. This was contrary to the promise Albany had made her – that she could see her son but with not more than four servants – and she protested loudly to his guards. A message was sent to the governor, Sir Patrick Crichton, to allow her to visit but his response was negative. He had received no orders from the council and therefore she could not be allowed in. Heartbroken and devastated at not seeing James, Margaret left the gifts and retired to her apartments in Holyrood.

It would be two months before she finally saw her son. In August a child at the castle came down with the plague and the young king was hastily moved to Craigmillar three miles away. Crichton didn't go with him and the keeper of Craigmillar, Lord Erskine, was more sympathetic to the plight of mother and son. He allowed Margaret access and finally she was able to see her seven-year-old alive and well, although shy at meeting her after nearly a year's absence. Before long James was moved back to Edinburgh. Some of the council still begrudged her contact with him and, given her previous flight to England, feared she would seize their king and escape with him. Fingers pointed at George Douglas, Angus's brother, as the man to execute such a plan and he was imprisoned without just cause.

Margaret moved to Newark Castle in Ettrick Forest to consider her position. She had hardly any support and no friends on the council except her husband. Lord Home, who had helped her flee to England, and his brother, had been executed in her absence. Whilst at Newark Angus brought her the news that in retaliation Home's kinfolk had murdered Sieur de la Bastie, Albany's deputy, on a trip to the borders. George Home had cut off the deputy's head and impaled it on a spike in the town of Duns. Goaded on by her husband, Margaret saw an opportunity to seize back the regency and make Angus the Deputy Governor. She hurriedly wrote to Dacre in September to send back Lord Home's brothers who she assumed he was sheltering:

> The Laird of Wedderburn hath prayed me to write to you, to send the Prior of Coldingham and George Home, for now is the time best for them, and cause them to promise you that they shall take our part, and be true to us. And, my good lord, remember that we had never so good a time for us, for either shall we have all the rule, or there shall be some trouble, so that you keep a good part to us and our friends if we need; for it were great shame that any other should have the rule afore us. I wot well that we will have many friends, on they may trust to be sure of England, as we think they should be, and as my trust is in you, and send me your counsel what we shall do.[8]

But Dacre would admit to nothing and advised Margaret to look to others for assistance. The help she sought from England would not be forthcoming until they heard Margaret and Angus had reclaimed the regency. But this was to prove difficult. The Scottish council gave James Hamilton, Earl of Arran, the position of deputy governor, much to their dismay, and although Angus was given a place on the council he refused to attend meetings, deepening the divide between the Hamilton and Douglas clans.

And now a deeper divide occurred between Margaret and her husband. She had forgiven him for not joining her in England. His excuse being that he had had to go to France on business for Albany. She had seen how he hankered after power and his failure to present their case at council meetings did her no favours. It seemed that he only wanted her for the authority she could give him and no more. She had no money. He was taking her rents from various properties but not providing her with anything to live on. Although Margaret was yet to find out, her monies were keeping his mistress.

She wrote to Henry in her misery:

I stand in a sore case, an I get not the king's grace my brother's help, and my lord cardinal's: for such jewels as his grace gave me at my departing from him, I am so constrained that I must put it away for money; and hath put away all my servants, because I have nought to give them, scantly to find me [with]. And had not been Robin Barton, comptroller, that hath laid out of his own purse five hundred pounds Scots, I had been fain to have lived a poor gentlewoman, and not like the woman that I am: for I am not answered of no part of my living, except Stirling and Linlithgow, and you know, my lord, what that is. And as for the forest of Ettrick and the earldom of March, I get nothing, nor of the lands of Methven. And, in good faith, since my last coming into Scotland, I have not gotten, of all the lands I have, four hundred pounds Scots...

But money wasn't the only issue:

The cause that I came hither most for was for the king my son's sake,
and I am holden from him like a stranger, and not like his mother,
which doth me great displeasure in my heart, considering I have no
other comfort here but him. Therefore, since they will not let me be
with my son, nor is not answered of my living, neither to the king
my brother's honour nor mine, I beseech his grace to let me come to
be in his realm...[9]

Dacre agreed Margaret was 'marvellous evil entreated, and no
promise kept unto her'[10] in a letter he wrote to Wolsey, yet Henry
was unmoved to help or to grant her permission to return to
England. At Christmas, Margaret moved to Tantallon, leaving
the Laird of Jedworth in charge of Newark. It was whilst here
that she finally had confirmation of her suspicions about her
husband. Not only was he taking her rents from her land and
properties at Methven and Ettrick Forest but he had forcefully
taken the house at Newark and was openly living with his
mistress and their child – at Margaret's expense.

Margaret asked the new deputy governor, the Earl of Arran,
to help her out. She had no one left to turn to in Scotland except
Angus's arch-enemy. Arran ordered Angus to leave Newark and
attend the council but he refused to budge. However she did
receive £2,000 of the £9,000 she was owed – a bittersweet victory
– since Angus was still demanding his rights to her income.
Previously Dacre had managed to get him to sign a bond that
appointed others to collect her rents thus ensuring she would
receive something but now Angus wanted to be released from
the bond and to collect the rents himself. His whole family
supported him but Margaret refused to make any changes to the
bond. She was poverty stricken and he had taken enough. If
Angus thought he could rule over her, he was mistaken. She was
of Tudor blood and the mother of the King of Scotland. With
steely determination, she vowed to put him behind her.

Would her brother, Henry, help her now? She wrote a long

letter to him in October 1518 detailing her situation:

As touching to myself, an it please your grace to wit how I am done to since my departing from you, it hath been very evil; howbeit, I was very loath to trouble your grace, and would not while I may no further that I see. I can get no reason, for I am not answered nor obeyed obeyed of my living, whereof I have not gotten two thousand pounds of Scotch money since my departing from your grace, which should be every year to me nine thousand pounds, and this is not to me to live in honour, like your sister, nor like myself ; which I beseech your grace to look well upon, and give no more credence to the fair words of the lords of Scotland, for it is to none effect. And, as for me, I have put off so long that I must give my jewels and such things as I got from your grace, for fault that I have nothing to spend, which will be great dis honour to me, and no honour to your grace, for I have no other to help me but you. And now it stands to me upon this point, I beseech your grace to help me, and to give me license to come into your realm; or else I will be put to the point to give my living at the pleasure of the duke and the lords, and they to give me what they please, which would be of little valour (value) to me. And please your grace to remember, the last writing I got from you, you bade me that I should not give over my conjunct feoffment for a sum of money, which I have kept. And your grace knows that you may of reason cause the ships of Scotland to be taken, and the goods in them, when they fail to me that I be not answered; which I have suffered too long, considering that your grace hath forborne so long to do any evil, and I am nought the better. Dearest brother the king, I trust your grace will not let me be overrun; and I wit well I will never get good of Scotland of fairness, nor I will never with my will bide here with them that I know well loves me not, which proves daily; and therefore do to me as ever your grace will, for all my weal is in your hands. Also please you to wit that I am sore troubled with my lord of Angus since my last coming into Scotland, and every day more and more, so that we have not been together this half- year.

Please your grace to remember that, at my coming now into Scotland, my lord Dacres and master Magnus made a writing betwixt me and my lord of Angus, for the surety of me, that he might not have no power to put away nothing of my conjunct feoffment without my will, which he hath not kept ; and the bishop of Dunkeld, his father's brother, and others his kinsmen, caused my lord of Angus to deal right sharply with me, to cause me to break the bond that he made to me, which I would not do ; and upon that he went and took up it that I live upon, and would not let none answer to me, and took my house of the new work (Newark), within the forest of Ettrick, which should be in the year to me four thousand marks, and I get never a penny; with much more evil that I shall cause a servant of mine to shew your grace, which is too long to write. And I am so minded that, an I may by law of God and to my honour, to part with him, for I wit well he loves me not, as he sheweth to me daily. Wherefore I beseech your grace, when it comes to that point, as I trust it shall, to be a kind prince and brother to me; for I shall never marry but where you will bid me, nor never to part from your grace, for I will never with my will abide into Scotland: and to send me your pleasure, and what your grace will do to me, for all my hope and trust is in your grace. I durst not send by land to your grace, for such causes as I shall cause you to understand, and I beseech your grace to write me your mind with this bearer, and God preserve you. At Edinburgh.[11]

Henry was immediately alarmed at Margaret's talk of Angus, and what was this about marrying again? In order to do that she would have to obtain a divorce and he was horrified that she would even contemplate it, although it would be something he would do himself in years to come. Discussing her predicament with Catherine, he decided to send the queen's priest Friar Bonaventure Langley again to talk to Margaret to urge reconciliation with her husband. Margaret later thanked Catherine for the loan of her priest but she had no intention of forgiving Angus.

She received letter after letter from her brother, his wife, Wolsey and Dacre but she refused to consider returning to her husband at this time. Why should she? He wanted everything from her and gave nothing back.

In February 1519, her financial difficulties were brought to the Scottish council. Margaret had come up with the idea of selling her dower lands back to the crown for an annual income but when she discussed it with Henry he dissuaded her. Now with no other alternative she brought her offer in front of the nobles. They chose to take back her lands at Ettrick for a yearly payment of 2,000 marks. Angus was furious. He sent Gavin Douglas before them with a declaration in protest saying 'my lord of Angus is spouse and husband to the queen's grace, by reason whereof he is lord of her person, dowry, and all other goods pertaining to her highness, and may dispose thereupon at his pleasure, according to all laws, and in especial the laws of this realm, here by me shewn and produced, by the which laws also her grace may follow nor pursue no action without his license'.[12] Not only did he not support her financially but he tried to stop her agreement with the council. They paid no mind to his protest though and Margaret won a small but satisfying victory.

In the autumn, sickness came to Edinburgh. When the deaths in the castle began to mount up, James was moved to Dalkeith and Margaret left for Stirling. By October the council were able to meet but the Earl of Arran, Deputy Governor, met with hostility from Angus and his supporters. Arran left to visit the young king and on his return found Angus had locked the gates of the city on him, putting his uncle Archibald Douglas in charge.

Around the same time Henry sent a different priest, Friar Henry Chadworth, to Margaret to convince her to return to Angus. He stayed for eight weeks during which time the Earl of Arran and the Archbishop of Glasgow tried to persuade her otherwise but the friar won out. What he said to make her change her mind is not recorded. He began by accusing of her of suspicious living but his words must have changed from accusation to reconciliation. Margaret had no wish to be back with such an unfaithful man as her husband but as she saw him rising in power she may have felt that only by reconciling with him would she get back control of her son.

Arran and his supporters were horrified and a delegation arrived at Stirling to inform her that if she went back to Angus she would lose their support, but she had made up her mind. She met up with her husband en route to Edinburgh where he accompanied her into the city with 400 horse and men. Angus's supporters were there in force including the Archbishop of St Andrews, bishops of Dunkeld, Aberdeen, and Murray, the earls of Huntley, Argyll, Ruthven, Morton, Glencairn, and Marshall, the lords Glamis, Hay, and Grey who 'with great triumph, in shooting of guns, and great melody of instruments playing, ... said she was welcome to the town'.[13] After their greeting, the first thing she did was to go to her son. Angus was so grateful to Henry for sending Chadworth to convince her to return to him, thus underlining his status, he wrote to the king of England 'her highness is full heartily appleased to resort and remain with me, her husband and servant, according and conform to all reason and laws, both of God and holy kirk'.[14] But Margaret was not right pleased to be with Angus. She just saw him as a means to an end and their relationship would never be what it once was. She knew he still kept his mistress and they would never be reconciled as husband and wife again.

Margaret caught smallpox in the winter and was severely ill. She heard Angus and his supporters were constantly harrying the other nobles, particularly those that supported the Earl of Arran. In April 1520, it came to a head in a skirmish that was to become known as 'Cleanse the Causeway' where the Douglas and Hamilton clans fought on the streets of Edinburgh. The Earl of Arran's brother, Patrick Hamilton, was killed along with 70 other men and the earl had to flee for his life. Angus was becoming all too powerful and when the Scottish council asked Margaret to write to King Francis I and Albany in France requesting his return, she willingly did so and also asked the duke to aid her in a divorce.

In June 1520, Albany was in attendance at the Field of Cloth of Gold, the momentous meeting between Henry VIII and Francis I. Amongst the celebrations and festivities, the situation in Scotland was discussed. Francis felt that the issues there could only be resolved by Albany's return. Henry did not agree. To make matters worse, Margaret's letter arrived as the kings were conversing. Henry continued expounding his objections but inside he was seething. His sister was nothing but trouble to him. As soon as he was free he ordered messengers to Dacre to try to talk her into sense. It was not Albany he wanted in control but her husband Angus. Francis saw that the time was not right to push Albany's return. Given Henry's current attitude, it would only result in hostilities between them and instead the duke was sent to Rome where amongst his other duties he could push for Margaret's divorce from Angus through the family connection of his sister-in-law who had married the pope's nephew.

Margaret received correspondence from Dacre that reminded her 'of what family you are'[15] as if she could ever forget. Her Tudor blood was everything to her but so was her son. Dacre continued on the matter of Angus 'You took him for your husband without consent of His Grace…and should go to him by the laws of God'[16] but their relationship at this point was far too broken to repair. It is not certain exactly when in 1520 Margaret finally broke with Angus and his followers but she soon returned to her former allies. Dacre reported 'Now of late, the Archbishop of St. Andrews, and all the lords being with her at supper, she stole away the same night out of Edinburgh, with six persons, three men and three women, with her, and within a quarter of a mile of the town, Sir James Hamilton, a bastard son of the Earl of Arran, which is deadly enemy to the Earl of Angus, having in his company one hundred horses, met her and conveyed her to Linlithgow, and from thence to Stirling, to the Archbishop of Glasgow, chancellor, and to the Earl of Arran, by whom she was counselled afore, when as friar Henry Chadworth was sent to her from the king's highness. And so she and the chancellor and the said Earl of Arran, being all together in company, returned back to Linlithgow'.[17]

Whilst there she continued to correspond with Albany and awaited his return. Although the French king could not allow his immediate departure the Scottish council informed him that he must be back by the 21st of August 1521 or he would forfeit the regency. Albany did not yet have permission to travel but he could send someone in his stead. Early in 1521, a French ship arrived in Scotland carrying the duke's friend, Gonzolles, with messages for both the council and Margaret. To the council, he sent assurances that he would arrive in Scotland by the stated date. He also ordered them to pay the queen's income and personally sent her funds from his own coffers to sustain her until they were forthcoming.

Henry could not believe that against all his advice and that of Dacre's and Wolsey's, Margaret was siding with Albany. Dacre had sent letter after letter to her warning her that if she stayed estranged from her husband and continued to support Albany's regency, she would receive no help from her brother. Sick of him telling her what to do, Margaret replied:

As to my Lord of Angus, if he had desired my company or my love, he would have shown him more kindly than he hath done. For now of late, when I came to Edinburgh to him, he took my house without my consent, and withheld my living from me, which he should not do of reason; nor that is not the way to desire my good will, and I to have taken both great displeasure of Scotland and trouble, and had no help of the king's grace my brother, nor no love of my Lord of Angus, and he to take my living at his pleasure and dispose it;

methinks, my lord, ye should not think this reasonable, if ye be my friend, as I trust ye be.[18]

But there was no sympathy for her from the English court. Wolsey wrote to Dacre 'albeit ye have given to her right, discreet, and sad counsel, yet she, being inveigled by the persuasions and advertisements of the Duke of Albany and his adherents, nothing regardeth her own honour, the surety of her son, nor yet of her husband or of herself'.[19]

It was with some relief that Margaret heard the duke had arrived on 18 November 1521. She hastened to meet him at Stirling, they continued on to Linlithgow and then to see James at Edinburgh. At the castle Albany was presented the keys but he passed them to Margaret. It was all that she could hope for – access to her son – and it was the duke that had granted it to her. So firmly was she in support of Albany that Wolsey and Dacre had gone into overdrive, sanctioned by their king, to spread rumours that Albany would marry Margaret after securing her divorce (though no mention was made of his own wife still living), usurp James V, and take the crown for himself. The Scottish council didn't believe a word of it and their reception of the duke was welcoming. Only the Douglas clan refused to acknowledge his return. They too were spreading rumours thick and fast to discredit both the duke and Margaret.

Albany had to deal with the Douglas faction. His first move was to remove them from office. He then called a Parliament who accused Angus and Gavin Douglas, Bishop of Dunkeld, of high treason. Angus went into hiding, probably sheltered by Dacre, somewhere along the borders whilst Dunkeld began his journey to the English court taking a list of complaints with him and seeking Henry's help. Margaret had asked that Angus be exiled rather than executed. Although Albany agreed, Angus could not be brought to heel just yet. Still he was in no position to trouble her and Albany had agreed to continue to petition Rome for her divorce. Margaret began to feel a sense of security. She would be rid of her husband and she now had access to her son. She would continue to look for peace between Scotland and England and began to compile a list of articles to be addressed that she would send to her brother.

Dacre was another matter. Once he had shown her friendship and support. Now he had turned against her. In December, she wrote a heated letter to the warden:

> *I commend me to you, and wit ye that my Lord Duke of Albany, governor of Scotland, is come for to do service to the king my son, and to the realm, and to help me to be answered and obeyed of my living, the which I have great need of, for there was never gentle-woman of my estate so evil entreated, and my living holden from me, as I have written oftentimes to you of before...*

She continued:

> *I know well ye have done your part to hinder me at the king's grace my brother's hand... My lord, I write sharply and plainly to you, for I have good cause, both for the king my son's sake and mine own; for ye have fortified my Lord of Angus against me, and counselled him to trouble me, in the contrary of the band that ye caused me to take of him, which ye would break again, which ye should not have done to your master's sister. And your answer, what shall be your part, that I and this realm may keep unto, and God keep you.[20]*

Dacre wrote a scathing reply and Margaret immediately complained to her brother that the warden had written 'right sharp'[21] to her. Henry, for the moment, was quiet on the matter.

Chapter Seven

Enter the King
1522–1523

Henry heard many wild rumours about his sister in January 1522. Dacre said Albany had threatened to kill him, that Margaret was bribing Angus to divorce her and he also hinted that Margaret and Albany had become lovers. Oblivious to the gossip around her, Margaret finished compiling her eight page list of articles to send to Henry in a bid to secure a lasting peace between their countries. She asked Dacre for a 40-day truce to cease hostilities along the border while she waited for Henry's reply, but he refused her request. Gavin Douglas, now at the English court, was muddying the waters and delivered up a 15-point memorandum against Albany. To add to the rumours, he set down accusations such as blaming the duke for Margaret's youngest son's death, being the key supporter of her divorce, keeping James V in poverty and taking treasury funds for his own use. Margaret wrote to Wolsey on hearing of his betrayal that Gavin Douglas was 'the cause of all the dissension in the realm'.[1]

Margaret had no real sense of her brother's displeasure until Thomas Benolt, Clarencieux King of Arms, arrived in Edinburgh on the 1 February with letters from the king. She had hoped that Henry would send words of peace and reconciliation but instead she was 'marvellously abashed'[2] at his invective against Albany and her seemingly untoward conduct. Reading her brother's rant stunned her into silence for many moments, while Clarencieux added to her shock by verbally underlining the king's words, telling her that Henry would no longer support her unless she changed her ways. She told the king at arms that Henry was listening to 'seditious and ill reports made and contrived against her, by very false persons'[3] and he was sent away to await her written reply to her brother.

Margaret must have thought long and hard about what to write. How could Henry believe in such slander without hearing her out first? She was his sister yet he trusted more in the men around him and the words of hatred coming from the Douglas clan. She told him:

> I think it will not be to your honour to suffer such false and untrue report made upon me, your sister. It had been your part, dearest brother, to have been my defender in all evil reports, and not to have alleged wrongously dishonour to me; which shall prove, of the self, false and contrary. And where that your grace alleges plainly, in your writing, that my mind is to marry the Duke of Albany, and desire the divorce to that intent, that was never in my intent, nor in his; as it will be well known. But I know the false information of the Bishop of Dunkeld; not the less he shall not be the nearer to his purpose, for I think never to take part with them that is contrary to the king my son, and his weal...

She continued to justify herself:

> I was constrained to make me friends, through my good bearing toward my lord governor of Scotland, wherein I have found me more kindness nor I have in any other in these parts. Suppose that your grace be displeased that I say this, I may say as I find cause hitherto; and if I did find the contrary, I should say it. But your grace may do to me, your sister, as ye please, but I shall make no evil cause, but it does me great displeasure in my heart of your unkindness.[4]

She wasn't the only one to receive letters from the king of England. Albany too received correspondence that accused him of a 'dishonest love' of Margaret and more ominously that he 'depart pleasantly, or bide the brunt of battle'.[5] Outraged he told

Clarencieux, 'I swear by the Sacrament that I might break my neck if ever I were minded to marry Her Grace, or do to her any shame or dishonour. I have enough with one wife. I greatly marvel that the King's Highness, upon light reports, would have the Queen his sister to be so openly slandered – as if I kept the said Queen as if she were my wife or my concubine! All my life, I will deny it'.[6]

Clarencieux, the king's man, also approached Parliament and they too were told of Henry's displeasure. The nobles stuck by Albany refusing to send him back to France as Henry wished and again all the ill rumours were refuted. As for little James V, he was being well looked after and Albany was not meddling 'with the custody of the King's person'[7] but leaving his care to Margaret – exactly what she had wanted. The council agreed with the statement Margaret had written – 'This country desires peace with England, if it can be had with honor, but will not consent to Albany's removal'.[8]

Clarencieux was sent back to the English court with verbal and written messages to impart. But to further their own position, the Scottish council sent a missive in the name of James V on 21 February denouncing Gavin Douglas as a traitor 'for having entered England contrary to the command of the governor, intending to reside there, and ordering the fruits of the bishopric to be sequestrated'.[9] But Henry continued to shelter him and support the Douglas clan including Angus. As far as the English king was concerned, Angus was married to his sister and should be ruling by her side if only Albany could be got rid of. But the duke's men had caught up with Angus, and Margaret's errant husband was exiled in March. One story tells of his refusal to go and subsequently being drugged at an inn and carted off, put on board a ship at Leith and taken to Dieppe. Whatever the truth Angus would find himself in France for many months to come.

He would arrive at a time when France was urging Scotland to go to war with England. The treaty of Rouen which renewed the 'auld alliance', although negotiated back in 1517, was ratified this year, tying Scotland and France closer together and agreeing a future marriage between James V and a daughter of France. Increasing hostilities would soon see Henry rallying his troops after signing a new treaty himself but with Charles V, the Holy Roman Emperor, to fight the French. In September, the king of England sent Charles Brandon, his sister Mary's husband, to Calais with 10,000 men with the aim of taking Boulogne. When the siege failed Henry ordered his men to head for Paris, the capital and Francis's seat of power feeling there was a 'good likelihood of the attaining of his ancient right and title to the crown of France to his singular comfort and eternal honour'.[10] But the troops sickened in the cold, many dying of frostbite, and Brandon, against his king's orders, returned home in disgrace.

Francis I, invoking the auld alliance, urged the Scots to invade England as they were invading his country. Albany reluctantly mustered 80,000 men to advance to the Scottish border where Dacre had stepped up his raids. Fearing a repeat of Flodden, Margaret asked Parliament to move James V from Edinburgh to Stirling for his safety. Content that her son was well protected, she asked Albany to sue for peace. When Dacre contacted her in August with the same idea, she rushed to the duke to beg him to negotiate a truce. The warden had realised that his English troops were vastly outnumbered by the Scots. The best fighting men had gone to France with their king and Dacre was in an uncomfortable position. He had no authority to arrange peace but craftily using Margaret as a go-between, he could blame her if it all went wrong. Margaret was well aware of his perfidy, but was still determined to be an 'angel of peace'.[11] It was always what she strived for, for herself, her son and for Scotland. It is said she rode out to the border to meet with Dacre personally to ensure a treaty was signed. The warden and the duke finally agreed to a month's truce and hostilities were averted. Whereas

Henry was angry with Dacre for exceeding his authority he agreed to the truce for the sake of his sister and peace in his kingdom. Francis I however was not impressed and Albany had to return to France in October to explain his actions or lack of them. Before his departure, the Archbishop of Glasgow, the Earls of Huntley, Argyle and Arran, and Gonzolles were agreed as regents to act in his stead until August the 14th of the following year.

Inadvertently, Henry had got what he wanted – Albany had left, giving him the opportunity to control Scotland once more. Margaret, no longer a thorn in his side, was now courted by her brother, Wolsey and Dacre in a flurry of letters that praised her peacekeeping efforts. Clarienceux. King-at-Arms, was sent to her again in November to compliment her on her conduct and to speak with the council about the duke's regency. He offered an extension of the truce until the following February but had also been authorised to make that 16 years if Scotland would refuse the return of Albany and sever their alliance with France for good. To sweeten the pot, Clarienceux was also to offer the hand of the Princess Mary to James V if the council acquiesced to Henry's wishes. As far as we know they only agreed to the extension of the truce. Albany was in contact with his regency nobles and under the auspices of Francis I was still preparing to return with French troops to wage war on England. He sent Margaret and the regents 1,000 French crowns each as payment to maintain their loyalty.

For the next few months the situation was unchanging; border raids continued, the council awaited Albany's return and Henry's plans came to nought. Margaret felt as if she was stuck between England and France. Who would help her now and see James V on the throne? Whilst Albany was away, it seemed that that might be her brother and she was determined to keep him on side for the time being. Around this time, she struck up a correspondence with the Earl of Surrey whom Henry had appointed lieutenant-general of the Scottish marches. In April 1523, she wrote:

> *I commend me heartily to you, and wit you I am informed that you are coming to the borders foments (over-against) Scotland; and there is a good friend and servant of mine which I am beholden to do for, which winnis (lives) in the border of Scotland, and nearest to your bounds of England, and is prioress of a poor abbey of sisters called Coldstream...*[12]

Margaret may have supported the prioress but on hearing of her double-dealing, plotting and reports to Albany about herself, she changed her tune and told Surrey to burn her out of her convent if she proved unfaithful to her. Surrey did take to burning but the prioress was safe for now. In June 1523, the English under his command raided Kelso, Eccles, Ednam and Stichell so savagely that Wolsey reported 'there is left neither house, fortress, village, tree, castle, corn or other succour for man'. The lords sent urgent messages for Albany to return.

Margaret's opinion of Albany changed with his absence. Now firmly supporting England, which would do nothing for her relationship with the Scottish lords, she wrote to Surrey '...you know how the lords are blinded with the duke of Albany, both for awe and for gifts of benefices...' (some of which she had received herself) and damning herself by her own words she continued with 'if the king's grace my brother's mind be to the weal and surety of the king my son, his nephew, as I trust firmly it be, he must shew it by one of these two ways, either by way of force, or by good entreating of the lords'.[13]

James was everything to her and she began to plan how he could take control of his birth-right. It was two weeks past the date Albany had set for his return. On the 31st of August, Margaret addressed Parliament on her son's behalf by reading out a letter in which he demanded his freedom from Albany's rule. The lords were loath to upset the boy who would soon come into his majority and debate ensued only to be interrupted by a messenger from Albany who assured them he was on his way. The boy king was to be kept at Stirling and the duke would return with French troops to invade England. The lords agreed they would wait two weeks for his arrival. James would be able to hunt and hawk within four miles of the castle but he would remain under the supervision of the Earls of Cassilis and Murray, the Bishop of Galloway, and the Abbot of Cambuskenneth at all times. Margaret tried in vain to change their minds but the decision was made.

Margaret furiously returned to writing letters urging her brother to appeal to the nobles to support her son. She planned to kidnap James whilst out hunting and have him appear in person before the council.

Wherefore, dearest brother, it is of force that you must cause the lords to leave the governor's ways, and by fair treaty or by very force; and this must be done in all haste, or else (the) king my son will be destroyed: considering now that the duke is forth of this realm, and the lords are not bound to him since our Lady-day of the Assumption, that was his promise to come. Now seeing that they are unbound, now is the time to change them, and to cause them to leave the governor's ways; and this I beseech your grace that it may be done in all diligence, for your honour and the weal and surety of the king my son.[14]

Henry's reply came in ordering Surrey to attack Jedburgh. Surrey wrote to Margaret that the attack could be used as a foil for her kidnap plan and that once she had James declared at Edinburgh, he would stop the hostilities on his orders and send men and money to her aid. Although Margaret had talked before of using force against the Scots, she wanted Henry's troops to take Edinburgh and force the nobles to her will. She never agreed with the border raids and this further act of violence appalled her.

In the end her plans came to nothing and as Surrey and his men burnt Jedburgh, the duke's ships were spotted along the coast. It was too late. Albany had arrived. He may have been late but he came with 4,000 French soldiers, new artillery and 600 horse. Margaret considered escaping over the border, wary of Albany's reaction to her after her attempt to free James. During her correspondence with Surrey it had been discussed several times and he had promised her assistance but privately he had written to Wolsey, 'Considering that I see no profit should come of her being here, but great costs and charges; wherefore, under the king's high correction and your grace's, methinks it were as profitable, and more good should come thereof, to have her remain in Scotland than to come into England'.[15]

After their period of courting Margaret in the hope that she would ensure English control, she no longer had as much value to them with Albany's return. The prioress of Coldstream reported that 'she is right fickle'[16] after an audience with the queen referring to her changing allegiances but Margaret didn't know who to trust and kept away from the duke whilst she still desperately tried to gain support from her brother and his councillors. Surrey was still writing to her seeking information about Albany's troops and movements. Foolishly, some would say, Margaret passed on sensitive details:

Now I will advertise you what he hath brought with him, and this I promise you is of truth: first, he hath eight-and-twenty cannons, and four double cannons that are far greater than any that was brought to Norham at the field; also he hath great pavasies going upon wheels with the artillery, to shoot and to break the hosts asunder, and of these he hath many, and every one of them hath two sharp swords before them, that none may touch them. They have by (besides) this, great number of smaller artillery of all sorts, and much powder, with all them that pertains to it; and twelve ships with victuals and wine.[17]

Wolsey at least was concerned for her safety. Surrey sent him copies of Margaret's letters which he characteristically wrote notes on. One such read 'It is not to be doubted but the Duke of Albany, intending to invade this realm, and having the queen in mistrust, will cause such watch to be laid upon her that she shall not now escape, though she would; and she had need beware what she writeth and speaketh, and to whom; for one such letter as this is, intercepted, might be her final destruction'.[18]

However Albany was well aware of Margaret's duplicity and made no move to curtail her plotting. He visited young James and assured him of his loyalty and meeting Margaret reassured her of his support. But his mind was firmly on invading England. On the 18th of October he met with the lords in Edinburgh and gave a rousing speech to goad them to war, reminding them of the losses they experienced at Flodden. Whilst Albany prepared to march across the border, Margaret joined her son at Stirling, to wait yet again for news of victory or defeat.

On the 1st of November, Albany laid siege to Wark Castle, a strategic border fortress, bombarding it with artillery for two days. When he ordered his troops across the River Tweed to take up the fight, the Scottish refused. Flodden was too raw to them and here they were taking up the battle not for themselves but for the French it seemed. Disgusted by their refusal, Albany sent 1,000 French men across in boats to attack the castle but they were repelled by its garrison. Hearing that Surrey was on his way with English reinforcements, a furious duke ordered their retreat saying 'I will give him no battle, for I have no convenient company to do so!'[19]

Disillusioned, Albany returned to Edinburgh and called Parliament to meet on November 18. It seems that now he was more aware of Margaret's reporting to the English and he would see her suffer for it. He ordered her to leave Stirling and her son's side and replaced his guardians with men he could be sure of. Margaret bemoaned 'I am put from the thing that I love the best in the world...' and rode out to face the lords with an unyielding rejection of their decree telling them 'I will let all Christian Princes wit that I am in great fear and dread touching his person'.[20] She returned to Stirling and refused to leave her son.

Albany and the lords were forced to attend her there at the beginning of December. When she asked what she had done to deserve such treatment, they replied that she was the king of England's sister and because of her prior escape across the border, they feared she would leave again taking her son and their king with her. The council was adamant. They would control her access to her son and those around him but Margaret could not be swayed to agree. The next day Albany tried a different tack and met with James V as well as his mother. Margaret wrote to Surrey of what transpired:

> he shewed to the king and me the order that was devised by the lords and him, touching such persons as should be about him, and prayed him and me to be contented therewith. The king said, it that was for his good he would be contented with; and I answered that I had shewn my mind before him and the lords, and therefore I could say no more then. I was warned that the governor had sent to fetch eight hundred of his Frenchmen...and that he was in purpose to take the king to another place, and to have put me from him.[21]

For the time being, Margaret had to accept their wishes, outwardly at least. As soon as she had finished her discussions with the council, she wrote down all her objections in front of witnesses 'revoking her concessions, as being made under the influence of fear'[22] that she sent to her brother. When she received no reply she bombarded Surrey with letters. It was to be a one-sided conversation for many months.

Stirling Castle

Chapter Eight

The Reign of James V
1524–1536

Albany was eager now to arrange a truce with England and allowed Margaret to stay with James during its negotiation. The duke and Wolsey struck up a correspondence to which Margaret was not included. Her previous role of mediator between their countries was overlooked. For Albany's part, the truce was a personal matter. Only if the situation was remedied in Scotland would he be allowed to return to France and his seriously ill wife. Finally in the spring of 1524 a truce was agreed until midsummer. Margaret was upset they had not consulted her and further put out by a lack of correspondence from her brother and Surrey. She wrote to the lieutenant-general 'I have written divers times to you since your departing from the borders, and has not gotten answer, nor no words from the king's grace my brother, nor from you, by the which I perceive that I am forgot with the king's grace and you, which is right displeasant unto me'.[1]

To add to her distress, she now heard a terrible rumour that her erstwhile husband Angus had been invited back to England by none other than her brother Henry. Albany took the opportunity to try to sway Margaret back over to his side. He could help her he said by offering her a home in France should Angus arrive back in Scotland, King Francis would give her a pension even if she chose to stay and James could marry a French princess thus confirming the auld alliance.

The conditions, written into a bond, somehow found their way to the English court. Margaret had left it with a trusty servant who was to find out what was happening regarding Angus's return and hearing that he was truthfully being courted by Henry was authorised to show it to the king in a bid to stop

Margaret's husband from being given permission to enter the kingdom. Dacre is thought to have intercepted it and added Margaret's seal, sending it to London as a done deal meanwhile writing to the queen in the strongest terms that by signing it she was betraying the king of England. Margaret immediately refuted that she had signed anything and the document was only to be seen by Henry to prove Albany wished her to side with France. She may well have wanted to use it to force her brother to support her but if so her plan backfired.

Once more Margaret was caught between Scotland, France and England with no true supporters and no real help from any quarter. But hope glimmered on the horizon, the council agreed the duke's request to return to France and in May 1524 he set sail with the assurance he would return in three months. He was in fact never to step foot on Scottish soil again. Albany gave control to the pro-French faction at court before he left and had tried to get an assurance from Margaret that she would not ally herself with England. Margaret would agree to no such thing. She saw a chance now to continue her original plan of freeing James from his guardians and making sure he finally took the reins of his kingship. And she would make alliances with whomever could support and forward her plan. The Earl of Arran and Beaton, now Archbishop of St Andrews headed the regency in Albany's absence with his fellow French man, Gonzolles, not as vice-regent this time, but as commander of Dunbar castle. It was to Arran Margaret now turned.

But then Margaret received a letter from her brother to officially inform her of what she had dreaded.

Our dearest cousin, the Earl of Angus, whom we find to be your obedient, loving, and faithful servant and husband ... hath secretly conveyed, first his brother, and afterwards himself, out of France; and, by far countries, not without great policy, be both now arrived and come unto our presence; intending and minding none other

thing but first to reconcile himself unto your grace and favour; and
secondly, to interpose his help, study, travail, and authority, to the
conducing of such good peace between us and that realm, as may be
for the weal and surety of the same[2]

Margaret's reply began with reminding him that what she did
now she did for her son and 'I beseech your grace to remember
well upon my last writings sent to your grace, and to make not
long delay in helping of the king my son, to put him to freedom
and out of danger of his enemies; for now is the time'. On the
matter of Angus she said:

Dearest brother, as to my lord of Angus and me, where your grace
desireth me to take him in my favour; as to that, he hath not shewn,
since his departing out of Scotland, that he desired my good will and
favour, neither by writing nor word, but now that he hath desired
your grace to write to me, knowing well that there is none that I will
do so much for as your grace; but I trust, dearest brother the king,
that your grace will not desire me to do nothing that may be hurt to
me your sister, nor that may be occasion to hold me from the king
my son, both for his weal and mine.[3]

The last thing Margaret wanted or needed was her husband's
return. On a personal level she had become attracted to Henry
Stewart, once head carver in her son's household she had risen
him up to become treasurer of her household; on a political level
she wanted her son placed firmly on the throne without any
interference. She sought support from Henry and the pro-
English faction at the Scottish court including her main ally the
Earl of Arran. As support from the Scottish nobles grew, Henry
agreed not to send Angus to Scotland just yet. With James V once
more as ruler, he would have some control through Margaret
and to keep her happy he sent money and a 200-strong
bodyguard to ensure her son took his rightful place as king.

Once more Margaret was being played, although for the time being her wishes were the same as her brother's.

Wolsey wrote to the Earl of Surrey, now styled Duke of Norfolk, 'the king and I think good that the Queen of Scots is to be used, as most propitious and convenient instrument in this matter, by all good ways possible, pretending that nothing shall be wrought but only by her means… For it is no folly for a good archer to have two strings to his bow, specially where as one is made of threads wrought by woman's fingers'.[4]

With English and Scottish backing, the 12-year-old King James escaped his French guardians at Stirling castle on 26 July 1524 and rode with Margaret into Edinburgh where the townsfolk came out to give him a rapturous welcome. In August, James supported by his mother, presided over Parliament to assert his rule and declare Albany no longer regent. He told them 'under penalty of the charge of treason, to break this treaty of Rouen, to deprive the Duke of Albany of his government, and renounce all their obligations to him'.[5] As the nobles came forward to give their oath of allegiance, Archbishop Beaton refused to reaffirm his loyalty telling James 'there is no man in your kingdom unwilling to obey you – but I entreat you to take better counsel'[6] maintaining that the Franco-Scots alliance should be upheld. Any dissenters were rounded up after the meeting and temporarily imprisoned for their pains.

Margaret was now in her element. Her precious son had his kingdom and she was there to act as regent and guide him and Scotland into the future supported by her brother and the English crown. She was delighted when Henry sent Archdeacon Magnus and Roger Radcliffe bearing letters of congratulation to herself and James, a gift of a jewelled sword for the king and news that Henry had made him a member of the Order of the Garter. For such a long time in her life, since the death of James IV, she had faced adversity and now she finally felt she had achieved her goal.

But her happiness was not to last. Henry allowed Angus to travel as far as Newcastle where he was to remain the guest of the Duke of Norfolk for the time being until Margaret could be persuaded to a reconciliation. Angus had written to Margaret assuring her of his loyalty but she had returned his letter unopened. It was now Magnus and Radcliffe who were charged with discussing his return but whilst they were broaching the situation with Margaret she received a messenger who told her that Angus had crossed the border. In fury she turned on the ambassadors who tried to placate her saying Angus had moved of his own volition, that Henry had not planned this and now Margaret as regent would have the upper hand anyway and could treat her errant husband as she saw fit. Seemingly mollified, Margaret was lulled into a false sense of security. Parliament confirmed her regency and she continued to return Angus's missives without reading them.

But her husband was not to be ignored. On 23 November at four in the morning Angus, living up to his nickname the Earl of Anguish, with men loyal to him such as the earls of Lennox and Buccleuch, scaled the walls of Edinburgh and opened the gates to 400 followers. They proclaimed they came in peace and were loyal to James V but wanted to assert their right to a place in Parliament. Margaret was roused from sleep to hear the disastrous news and immediately ordered the cannon atop the castle to be aimed at the men. Magnus appalled by such hostility urged Margaret to speak to her husband. She railed against him and told him to 'go home and not meddle with Scottish matters'[7] then the cannon fired. Unfortunately four innocent people were killed but it forced Angus to retire to Tantallon.

Margaret blamed Henry for allowing her husband to return to Scotland thus endangering her son's life. She wrote to him:

> I think your grace should not have…put the king my son in danger
> of his person, as he hath been now lately through the said earl of

Angus coming in the manner he came within the night... And now this realm may understand that your grace hath sent in the earl of Angus to do me displeasure, and to hold me in trouble daily...Not the less it is right unkindly that your grace (hath) done this to me your sister...[8]

Henry for once agreed. He would no longer support Angus fearing he had his own motives and may have been paid by France to force Margaret away from England and back to France. Although a standoff ensued between Margaret and her husband, the French certainly took the opportunity to try and persuade her back to their alliance with a present of 30,000 crowns.

Magnus reported to Henry in January 1525 that Margaret had rejected overtures from the French. In fact Margaret was increasingly concerned at the support her husband was mustering and she continued a correspondence with Albany to help her attain a divorce telling him she could do more against Angus if they were legally separated. She called a council meeting for the 23rd, but Angus, Beaton and more than 40 other nobles refused to attend and held their own meeting two weeks later. Margaret's authority was crumbling. Even her main ally the Earl of Arran was rarely to be seen. She asked Henry to send her 10,000 men to protect herself and James but they were not forthcoming. Beaton produced a pamphlet outlining her misrule and there was rising discontent at the way the country was being run. As Angus became more popular, Margaret saw that she needed to take steps to avert a civil war in Scotland yet she still wanted to safeguard herself from her husband. She offered him 10,000 marks if he would agree to their divorce but he made no reply. To placate him, she next offered him entry to Edinburgh and an invitation to attend the next Parliament on 23 February.

With an agreement to safe conduct her husband returned to Edinburgh with a show of force. 'About midnight, long files of troops, headed by the Earls of Angus and Lennox, marched into the city, and quietly retired to their lodgings. On the morrow, the remaining lords made their entrance, with 2000 horsemen, well armed and mounted, belonging rather to the class of yeomanry than of common soldiers. They all took the precaution to locate themselves beyond the reach of gun-shot from the castle'.[9]

The opening of Parliament was an outward show of accord. James V accompanied by his mother led the procession to the Tolbooth with Angus carrying his crown, Arran his sceptre and Argyll the royal sword. There it was agreed that Margaret could remain with her son at Holyrood and a peace truce with England would be renegotiated by a new regency council that gave positions to the nobles who had opposed her. For some it was believed Margaret had agreed too readily to allow Angus back but behind the scenes she was writing to Albany and Francis I to plead her case for divorce and ask them to urge the pope to grant her wish. Only then did she feel she could rise up against her power-hungry husband. She must have hoped that her brother would support her but when Henry found out she had been corresponding with the French he was furious. Magnus was charged with delivering the king's reprimand to her. After reading the first few lines she burst into tears and cried 'such a letter hath never been written to any noblewoman'.[10] Henry had made the point of informing her that Francis I had been captured at Pavia and her hopes for a divorce any time soon were dashed. She had agreed with Angus that they would not resume life as husband and wife until Whitsuntide only because she had felt sure he would no longer be her husband by then. Her affair with Henry Stewart had continued but he was a married man and seeking his own divorce. It was obvious their relationship was not just a flirtation and many were angered by her affiliation with the rapid advancement of a man so beneath her. Margaret had taken him with her to Holyrood but for safety's sake she now had him moved to Stirling. Margaret's brother especially was ashamed at her behaviour and felt her open adultery made him the talk of the European courts just at a time when Henry was negotiating the Treaty of the More with France that would keep Albany from ever returning to Scotland.

Margaret's world was fast dissolving into chaos. When Angus illegally granted his brother a bishopric she used it as an excuse to absent herself from court and retire to Stirling, her fortified dower castle. She stayed away from the July meeting of Parliament but it was a fateful move on her part. It gave the nobles a chance to strip her of any remaining power she had including the guardianship of her son. It was decided that as before James's care would be delegated to certain men loyal to the crown on a rotating basis four times a year with Angus taking the first charge. When it came time for a change in guardianship, Angus refused to relinquish control and in effect gave himself full power over the king and Scotland.

In this he had overreached. The tide began to turn against him and Margaret found herself once more with supporters and once more with the Earl of Arran at her side. She herself had ridden into the north to gather men to try and free her son from Angus' clutches. In January 1526, she was making her way to Linlithgow where those who opposed Angus were gathering when she heard her husband was also on his way to stop the rebels with 7,000 men and James V himself at the head of them. Margaret retreated before their troops met to plan her next move.

In June, Parliament declared that at the age of 14, James V was now old enough to rule but Angus was still very much in control. No one could get to the boy least of all Margaret. Angus forced the young king to announce that he was content and happy with the arrangement and made a great show of taking James everywhere with him. In secret he managed to get letters to his mother telling her of his true situation. A failed attempt to free him in July was organised by Margaret and the Earl of Lennox. Not to be thwarted, the earl tried again a few weeks later but was killed in a skirmish against Angus and his men. James watched in horror as this loyal man perished. The earl had taken the boy into the fray to teach him a lesson and to prove that his mother would fail in every attempt to regain control of her son. He continued to lay siege to Stirling castle forcing Margaret and her lover to flee.

To exert Angus's authority Margaret was asked to attend November's Parliament. She went with the sole purpose of being able to see her son and was duly met by James and her husband in a cordial welcome. Angus would allow her access to the king only if she agreed with him in all things, fail him and she would face exile. Margaret could do nothing but agree and thus having acquiesced she was able to spend the next few months enjoying her son's company but it would be James who would cause her to leave Edinburgh in the spring of 1527.

Margaret asked that Henry Stewart be allowed to court. If he hadn't already heard the rumours, James had been made aware of his mother's lover through correspondence with Wolsey. Henry VIII was still trying to persuade her from a divorce and to keep the peace to remain married to Angus. James refused his mother's request. It would not be seemly to have the man at court and their affair openly flaunted when they were both still married to other spouses. Margaret lost her temper. She had been through so much and Henry Stewart was her consolation. In a rage she swore she would leave for France unless she could be with Stewart but James, probably spurred on by Angus, had no intention of backing down. Margaret, after this heated quarrel with her son, instead left for Stirling.

She would not find out until December that in fact in February her divorce had been granted and for all these months she had been a free woman. And her brother Henry for all his posturing and demands was indeed seeking a divorce himself. Margaret wasted no time in preparing for her next marriage and she wed her lover Henry Stewart, son of Lord Avondale who had died at Flodden, in March 1528 but there was no happy honeymoon period. Henry wrote to her 'that for the weal of your soul, avoid eternal damnation...Relinquish the adulterous company of him that is not, nor may not be, of right, your husband'.[11] No congratulations there and Angus immediately rode out to Stirling with James when they heard the news. William Dacre, who had taken over as Warden of the North Marches after his father's death, wrote to Wolsey:

> As for news of Scotland, Henry Stewart has married the queen of Scots, as she hath confessed herself; and for that cause the king her son caused the Lord Erskine and a certain company to lie about the castle of Stirling to attack him; and thereupon the said queen delivered him out, and so he is put in ward by the king's commandment.[12]

Although Dacre felt it was James who had ordered the attack on Stirling it was Angus who had initiated it, incensed that he would no longer have access to Margaret's money and lands. James was increasingly unhappy about being in Angus's control and was seeking a way to escape his clutches. The opportunity came when he was left in the care of James Douglas of Parkhead at Falkland. Telling his warder that he needed to go to bed early so to rise for hunting in the morning, he waited until the palace had settled down for the night and slipped out to the stables. Unchallenged he mounted a horse and rode hard for Stirling. Soon all the nobles that were unhappy with Angus's reign joined him there. Once the Douglas's realised they had lost control of the king an attempt was made to follow him to Stirling but backed by an increasing swell of loyal men, James banned them from coming within seven miles of court and his person. Finally the young king had escaped his guardians and Margaret was triumphant.

Angus and his supporters retreated to Tantallon and could do nothing as James jubilantly rode into Edinburgh, his mother by his side, backed by many nobles including Argyll, Arran, Bothwell, Eglinton, Montrose, Moray and Rothes to finally take control as king. For the first few weeks James remained in fear of the Douglas's, keeping a guard outside his rooms at all times whilst they raided along the borders causing as much upheaval as they could.

In September, Parliament met and Angus was formally accused of treason and of keeping the king against his will. A bounty of 100 marks was placed on his head and 40 marks would be given for the capture of his uncle or brother. Wary that Henry VIII would defend his previous ally, James wrote to his uncle to tell him 'that if Angus or his adherents seek help in England it may be refused'.[13] Henry pressed for Angus to be pardoned but James would never forgive him.

Margaret surprisingly was more ambivalent. As long as Angus stayed far from Edinburgh and the centre of power Margaret would be content. She declared 'We, moved of pity, and having considerations of the time present, not only for the weal of the Earl of Angus, but first for the merit of God...make openly known that we bear no rancour to the said earl...'[14] Margaret had got what she had always wanted – her son on the throne – and her new husband had been made Lord Methven with lands and title of his own. She was in a secure and happy place and could afford to be magnanimous. She also had need to appease Angus who had taken their daughter, Margaret Douglas, into his care against her wishes and 'would not suffer our own daughter to remain with us for our comfort'.[15] Their daughter would eventually be welcomed at Henry's court and Margaret's main aim now was to ensure that a peace treaty was renewed between Scotland and England which was duly signed in December. Once again Margaret and Henry were in accord. Magnus wrote of her:

I have not at any time found the Queen of Scots more inclined to the devotion of England, or to the pleasure of her dearest brother, the king's highness, than her grace is at this season; desiring none other thing but unity, concord, and amity, to continue between both the kings and their realms; and being in right good favour; as nature requireth, with the king's grace her son, she is clearly given to the advancement, furtherance, and setting forward of the same.[16]

Margaret would spend the next years entirely devoted to James. In the summer of 1529 she accompanied him on his summer progress into the Highlands where the Earl of Atholl spent £3,000 on their entertainment including the building of a temporary palace constructed in a beautiful meadow. They spent their days hunting in the surrounding countryside and it was estimated that over 600 animals were killed for their pleasure. As they left the palace was torched which concerned the papal nuncio travelling with them but James explained it was the custom to burn the lodgings of guests once they had departed. As the years passed peacefully Margaret also presided over the entertainments for the English embassy in 1531 and accompanied James on a hunting trip to her estate in Ettrick Forest in 1532.

Enjoying these peaceful times to the full what Margaret failed to notice was her son's growing hostility towards England. Henry had allowed Angus and his supporters to cross the border and they had continued to send out raiding parties into Scotland. Not only that but James found out that Henry was paying Angus £1,000 a year to keep him loyal to him. Whilst James and Henry bristled at each other, Margaret tried to keep the peace sending her brother 'gentle letters' although Henry called her 'the mother of our enemy'.[17] It seems the French ambassador Beauvais took part in cooling frayed tempers and hostilities were averted.

Henry was much caught up over the next months with his divorce from Catherine of Aragon and his marriage to Anne Boleyn in January 1533. When his personal difficulties died down he sent commissioners to Margaret to arrange a meeting between himself and James. It was the first time he had contacted Margaret in months, ignoring her previous requests to visit

England, but she was delighted to be involved and made it her goal 'to see our most dearest brother and our most dearest son, in proper personages together, and of one loving mind'.[18]

She immediately sent for James but he wasn't as eager for the meeting as his mother. Several of his council thought it a bad idea and leaders of the Scottish church were still reeling from Henry's break with Rome and felt it unwise to meet with a heretic king.

Not to be put off and determined to convince her son Margaret sent Henry a placatory letter in December 1534:

> ... *your desires is completely granted by our dearest son, most pleasantly, heartily, and tenderly; as, by his report made to your said ambassadors, they will inform you more large. Moreover, our dearest son has affectionately desired us write in his name unto you these words following, that not only will he meet, and commune, and visit you, but also loves your grace better than any man living next himself, and will take your part, his person and his realm, against all living creature under God, without you first fail unto him, which he trusts never shall be.*

Not exactly truthful but Margaret was in full flow. She also reflected on their past relationship:

> *Please your grace, howbeit in times by past some misadvised persons made unkindly reports of us unto you, without cause or offence in us, we have, and always shall, endure it, and continue your most loving, kind, and faithful sister, intending no less all time of our life, having such confidence in you that you will hold us the same. Your grace is our only brother, and we your only sister; and since so is, let no divorce nor contrary have place, nor no report of ill-advised (persons) alter our conceits, both brotherly and sisterly love ever to endure, to the pleasure of God and weal of us both; and trust no less in me than in yourself, in all and sundry things at our*

whole power, as pleaseth your grace command.[19]

Mary Tudor had died in 1533 and Margaret and Henry were the last of Henry VII's children. Margaret had ever been a princess of England and as she was now in her forties her relationship with her brother was something she mulled over. All she wanted was peace between the kingdoms, to be one happy family, but Margaret was ever blinkered when it came to her son. The power she once had had dissipated. She no longer took part in council meetings and James V was in his element. Still she continued to press for a meeting between her brother and son and finally in 1536 James agreed to meet Henry.

But it wasn't going to be easy. Whilst Henry had suggested York, James wanted to meet in Newcastle. James also wanted to know what was on the agenda and refused to discuss the Douglas's. He also had no intention of discussing religion or supporting Henry as Supreme Head of the Church of England. His misgivings layered upon layer. Margaret still hoping for a successful outcome spent £20,000 on clothes but James' reluctance to travel to England continued and in the end brought outward refusal. He turned on his mother accusing her of trying to get him on English soil to face his enemy. Their argument was fraught and upsetting. Margaret knew now that her son was far beyond her control or influence and was heard to say 'I am weary of Scotland'.[20]

She turned back to her brother and suggested in July that she come to England to meet with him instead but Thomas Cromwell scornfully wrote to her that she would not be welcome without her son. She also tried for funds to reimburse her for the outrageous sum she had spent on a meeting that would never happen. It was no time to ask Henry for anything. Anne Boleyn had been accused of adultery and executed on 19 May. Her brother was in no mood for Margaret's wants and needs and tersely wrote 'You must not ask me to disburse notable sums merely because you are my sister'.[21]

He had also been troubled by her daughter Margaret
Douglas. He had welcomed her to court when she first arrived in
1530 and provided her with rich gowns, clothing and gifts to
befit a child of Tudor blood. By October 1533, she had joined the
Princess Mary's household and later was one of Anne Boleyn's
ladies. Whilst there she met and fell in love with Anne's uncle
Thomas Howard, a family now much in disgrace. When Henry
heard they had secretly married he had them both thrown in the
Tower of London. Thomas was condemned to death but was
spared only to live the rest of his life in incarceration.

Margaret had ever loved James as her favourite child and we
don't know how much it pained her to be parted from her
daughter when Angus took her across the border. It must have
been a comfort to know that she was at least safe at her brother's
court and would enjoy an upbringing as sumptuous as hers had
been. Margaret has been slated for not appearing to care for her
only daughter but as soon as she heard of her troubles she wrote
to Henry pleading for leniency:

*Please you understand we are in formed lately that our daughter
Margaret Douglas should, by your grace's advice, promise to marry
lord Thomas Howard, and that your grace is displeased that she
should promise or desire such thing; and that your grace is resolved
to punish my daughter and your near cousin to extreme rigour,
which we no way can believe, considering she is our natural
daughter, your niece, and sister natural unto the king our dearest
son, your nephew ; who will not believe that you will do such
extremity upon your own, ours, and his, being so tender to us all
three as our natural daughter is. Dearest brother, we beseech your
grace, of sisterly kindness and natural love we bear, and that you
owe to us your only sister, to have compassion and pity of us your
sister, and of our natural daughter and sister to the king our only
natural son and your dearest nephew; and to grant our said*

daughter Margaret your grace's pardon, grace, and favour, and remit of such as your grace has put to her charge. And, if it please your grace, to be content she come in Scotland, so that in time coming she shall never come in your grace's presence. And this, dearest brother, we, in our most hearty, affectionate, tender manner, most specially and most humbly beseech your grace to do, as we doubt not your wisdom will think to your honour, since this our request is dear and tender to us, the gentlewoman's natural mother, and we your natural sister, that makes this piteous and most humble request.[22]

Margaret had asked that her daughter be sent back to her but Henry had no intention of sending her back to Scotland. As her daughter's health deteriorated, the young Margaret wrote to Cromwell forsaking Thomas Howard and her love for him. Their marriage had not been consummated and so she was still marriageable. She was also still written into the succession and too valuable to be allowed to languish alone for long. Henry had her sent to the nuns at Syon Abbey and she would stay there out of favour and in disgrace for the next year.

James also had given Margaret cause for concern. The time had come for her son to be married. He had already fathered five illegitimate children and his mother amongst others gauged it was time to settle him down and make a political alliance. Although he no longer listened to her, Margaret pressed for a match with her brother's daughter, the Princess Mary, although she had now been bastardised by her father's divorce and the new act of succession. From France, the Duke of Albany suggested marriage to Catherine de Medici. James himself had wanted to marry his mistress – causing another falling out with his mother – but now favoured a French match as previously agreed in the Treaty of Rouen. Francis I, King of France, offered three choices Marie de Guise, Marie de Bourbon and Isabelle of Navarre but not his daughter, the Princess Madeleine as James had hoped. Initially it was agreed he would marry Marie of Bourbon and Albany, in his last act for Scotland, signed the marriage contract on James' behalf. The duke was by now suffering with his health and retired to his home at Mirefleur where he died in June.

James set sail for France a month later but was forced back by bad weather. In September conditions had improved and he left to find a bride and the new queen of Scotland leaving Margaret as regent for the last time.

Chapter Nine

The Final Years
1537–1541

Margaret's regency was relatively peaceful but her personal life was falling apart. In January 1537 she found out that her husband Henry Stewart, Lord Methven, had been stealing the rents from her properties and not only that but he had housed his mistress Janet Stewart, daughter of John Stewart, 2nd Earl of Atholl and Lady Janet Campbell, in one of her properties and was raising a young family. Margaret immediately began to plan for divorce and as always turned to her brother with her troubles.

James was still in France and she felt ignored and unwanted. She complained he had left her without money or protection. The council didn't listen to her any more. She was a thing of the past and mostly forgotten. She had written over and over to Henry but he rarely replied. He had finally found a wife in Jane Seymour who made him happy, and was looking forward to the birth of their first child later in the year. For his part he never really knew the truth of Margaret's situation and was getting conflicting reports from his envoys. Eventually he did write back to her many letters, coining Methven with the nickname 'Muffin':

We should be sorry if our good brother and nephew your son should use you otherwise than a son should his mother. As it appears by Cambell's credence that you are well handled and grown to much wealth and quiet and Berwick's credence is quite to the contrary we are in doubt which to believe. Also having heard at other times from you of your evil treatment by your son and Lord Muffyn, and as we are sending the bearer into those parts on our business; we desire you to show him the "points wherein you note yourself evil handled," and whether you desire us to treat of them with your son, or only generally to recommend your condition.[1]

He sent Ralph Sadler to find out more with £200 to tide her over. Margaret complained to the envoy that 'Though I be forgotten in England, I shall never forget England'[2] but when Sadler returned to the English court and confirmed Margaret's difficulties, he was immediately sent over to France to talk to James. Although Henry lost his patience with his sister many times and their relationship would ever be fraught, he did provide for her when it suited him – she was still family after all.

Her son had not married Marie of Bourbon as planned but Francis I's daughter Madeleine of Valois on 1 Jan 1537 at Notre Dame. Originally reluctant to see his fragile daughter become a bride, Francis had finally consented to the marriage and the newlyweds had spent the last few months being entertained at the French court. James was at Rouen preparing to return home when Sadler arrived and was shocked to hear of his mother's predicament. He wrote to her and to the council and Methven demanding they sort out her financial affairs.

Somewhat appeased Margaret awaited her son's return. A secret envoy from Henry visited her and found her still convinced she should divorce her husband. Methven was spreading the rumour that she would remarry Angus and others said that she had taken a fancy to John Stewart of Arran but there was no truth in the gossip. Margaret wanted a divorce and then hoped that Henry would allow her to spend the rest of her days in England. This she needed to discuss with her son.

James arrived back in Leith on 19th May with his new wife. Francis I had asked Henry VIII for permission for the couple to return through England but although he agreed Madeleine could journey across his kingdom, James was forbidden. Arriving then by ship, Madeleine made her entrance by kneeling on the shore and, lifting a handful of sand, she kissed it. Scotland had a new queen and there was great rejoicing for days. Margaret, now

Queen Dowager, mentioned her divorce predicament and James was initially agreeable especially since she had bribed him with her estate at Dunbar but any further talk of Margaret's needs was put off by Madeleine's poor health. The 16-year-old, who was probably already suffering from tuberculosis, took to her bed in Holyrood Palace while James sent for her French doctor but she never rallied and weeks later on 7th July she died.

It was the wrong time to press her son about her divorce but she went ahead and James, now fearing she would return to Angus, absolutely refused. She wrote to tell Henry that she had found 24 'famous folk'[3] to back up her claims against Methven and that her divorce and petition was about to be granted but whether Henry supported her or not, James would not ratify any divorce in Scotland. They argued long and hard until Margaret left court and in her pain and rage headed for the border. She didn't get far before his men caught up with her and took her to Stirling Castle. She would later write to Cromwell of her unhappiness 'I shall never have another husband, and unless I get some remedy I shall pass to some religious place, and bide with them...The King my son is more unkind to me daily, and I had liever be dead than treated as I am'.[4]

Margaret could not get through to her son. He was more concerned with his vendetta against Angus and his family. On 17 July 1537, James ordered the execution of the earl's sister, the Countess of Glamis. She was accused of witchcraft but there was no evidence against her until her servants and family were tortured and made to admit to false charges. James made her death a gruesome spectacle by burning her at the stake in Edinburgh Castle whilst her young son was made to watch. His actions must have horrified Margaret but we hear nothing from her during this period.

She was still at Stirling in December when she wrote to Henry to tell him that James was making preparations for his next marriage and was sending his secretary to inform him of the details. Henry too was considering his next marriage after Queen Jane had died in October shortly after giving birth to their son Prince Edward. Both of the kings were eager for the hand of the recently widowed Marie de Guise. She had proved her fertility by bearing two male children and would provide a strong alliance with France, something that Henry was now eager for but Marie wasn't so keen on the English king. When told of Henry's interest and his comments that he needed a big wife referring to her tallness, Marie is reported to have said 'I may be big in person, but my neck is small'.[5] Who wanted to risk being the next queen for Henry to behead? Her family may have thought otherwise. It was certainly more prestigious for their daughter to become the queen of England rather than Scotland but Francis was wary of the powerful Guise dynasty and since Marie had already been proposed as a suitable bride for James, he decided that she would become the next Scottish queen. To appease her parents he provided a dowry of 150,000 livres and gave Marie the honorary rank of Daughter of France.

A proxy wedding was held at Notre Dame in Paris on 18 May 1538 to which James sent Lord Maxwell as his representative accompanied by over 2,000 of his lords. Marie's youngest son had since died but she tearfully said her goodbyes to her surviving son by the Duke of Longueville, knowing she would probably never see him again. After the ceremony and feastings, the nobles accompanied Marie back to Scotland arriving on 10 June at Crail in Fife. James rode out to meet her and escort her back to St Andrews where she was met by the Scottish nobility. Although the celebrations were not as lavish as for Madeleine, Marie still enjoyed a royal welcome. At the New Abbey Gate, a mechanical cloud descended and opened to reveal an angel who 'having the keys of all Scotland in her hands, (and) delivering them to the Queen's grace in sign and token (showed) that all the hearts of Scotland were open to the receiving of her Grace'.[6] After their marriage was blessed, James took Marie on a tour of his palaces, recently restored and refurbished before she settled into court life. James had loved the chateaus of France and a love of architecture was something they would share as the palaces of Linlithgow and Falkland were added to in the Renaissance style over the coming years.

Margaret had once again asked her brother to supply her with money for new gowns for her son's wedding to which he had not responded, still she wrote to him diligently whether he replied or not. She seems to have got on well with her new daughter-in-law writing to Henry in July, 'Your Grace shall understand that the King my dearest son is in good health and prosperity, and the queen his wife, and great love betwixt them, and great honor done to her, and she is right richly come here in this realm...I trust she will prove a wise Princess...I have been much in her company, and she bears herself very honourably to me, with very good entertaining'.[7] Her divorce forgotten she had made amends with both her son and her husband whom she was living with again. Her brother, spurned by Marie, married Anne of Cleves on 6 January 1540 at Greenwich but by July had had the marriage annulled.

Margaret entered into a quiet period of her life now. It appears she became more pious or at least enjoyed the company of the devout Marie. Norfolk reported 'the young Queen is all papist, and the old Queen nearly as much so'.[8] She wrote to Henry asking he allow the safe passage of a Catholic monk through his kingdom at a time when others were being persecuted. Henry was enjoying his new wife, the teenage Catherine Howard but he would find no peace, whereas Margaret was content to live out her older years with her family. She became a grandmother with the birth of James, Duke of Rothesay born in May 1540 and Robert, Duke of Albany who followed in April 1541. But tragically both boys died within days of each other in the same month although they were living in separate households. Their passing caused their parents great sorrow and Margaret was there as a comfort and support. Although her correspondence with her brother Henry was less these days she wrote:

Pleaseth you, dearest brother, here hath been great displeasure for the death of the prince and his brother, both with the king, my dearest son, and the queen his wife; wherefore I have done great diligence to put them in comfort, and is never from them, but ever in their company, whereof they are very glad. Herefore I pray your grace to hold me excused, that I write not at length of my matters at this time, because I can get no leisure... [9]

By September, it seemed that Margaret would get her longed-for wish and that James and Henry would finally meet at York. Both set out for the meeting with Henry arriving ahead of James and ordering a magnificent reception. James got as far as the border and changed his mind leaving Henry to impatiently wait for his nephew. When the English king realised the Scottish king was not going to show up he was furious and ordered the Duke of Norfolk to ravage the border lands. Margaret was never going to see peace between her son and her brother.

Margaret's troubles had made her ill and she took to her bed in October at Methven castle. It appears that she suffered a stroke but did not consider that she was dying. She made no will and at first refused the insistence of her priests to prepare for death. But as the hours passed she realised she would not recover. James, who was at Falkland, was sent for and as he rode to his mother's death bed she surprisingly told the priests 'to beseech the King to be gracious to the Earl of Angus' and tell James to look out for his half-sister, Margaret Douglas and pass on her jewels. Slipping into a coma she died on 18 October at the age of 52. James had not made it in time to say his goodbyes.

Her son arranged a grand and fitting funeral for her at the Carthusian Abbey of St John in Perth attended by the Scottish nobility but he did nothing about her dying wishes. The Earl of

Angus would never be forgiven and the jewels and 2,500 marks she left to his half-sister reverted to the crown. The English ambassador reported Margaret's death and final words to Henry later in October. No record is made of his reaction. Of Henry VII's and Elizabeth of York's children, he was the last to survive.

Even in death Margaret knew no peace. Hers had been a troubled existence, torn between Scotland and England, her husbands, son and her brother. Margaret's third husband Lord Methven married his mistress Janet Stewart, not long after the queen's death and they had four children before his demise in 1552. The abbey she was laid to rest in, also the burial place of James I, was ransacked during the Scottish Protestant Revolution of 1559 and her tomb destroyed. Her remains were burnt and her ashes were scattered around the grounds. A sad ending for a once magnificent Tudor princess.

Henry VIII

Chapter Ten

Margaret Tudor's Legacy

The relationship between Margaret's son and her brother never did improve. As a king, James was known to be authoritative, stubborn and unyielding. He was a devoted Catholic and would never be persuaded to support Henry's break with Rome. He governed as he thought fit, controlling the treasury and the crown estates and acting judicially sometimes to the detriment of his nobles gaining him the moniker of being 'ill-beloved' but he also went amongst his people and acted as he deemed just and fair when dealing with their complaints and so was also known as King of the Commons.

Henry, like his nephew, was much the same in personality, stubborn and wilful. By 1542, the English king was planning another fighting foray into France. To keep James busy and prevent him invading England whilst he was gone he ordered Sir Robert Bowes, Warden of the East Marches, and his men including the Earl of Angus, Margaret's second husband, to harry the Scottish borders. James retaliated by placing George Gordon, 4th Earl of Huntly, in charge of his troops to defeat the English at Haddon Rig. To push his advantage, the Scottish king sent an army of around 18,000 men to cross the border region into Cumbria. They met the English, only 3,000 strong, under the command of Sir Thomas Wharton, on 24 November 1542 at Solway Moss. James was not with them but at Lochmaben Castle where he was ill with a fever. As his illness worsened he moved to Falkland to wait for news. He should have been victorious – his army vastly outnumbered the English – but his soldiers ran amok without clear guidance from their leaders and were caught between the river Esk and bog land, hundreds drowning and many more taken prisoner, before they surrendered.

The Scottish king was deeply humiliated and also severely ill. His reign ended when he died just weeks later at the age of 30 on 14 December leaving behind his wife Marie de Guise with a two-week-old daughter who had been born at Linlithgow in his absence. This little girl, Margaret's granddaughter, was Mary, Queen of Scots. Against Marie's wishes, the Earl of Arran, whom she felt was 'the most inconstant man in the world'[1] was made regent and placed in charge of her care. He negotiated a peace treaty with Henry VIII and a marriage treaty for Mary to marry Henry's son, Edward, although this would not come to pass.

King Henry VIII didn't get to France until 1544 where his siege of Boulogne was successful but age and poor living was catching up with him. Henry had allowed his sister's daughter, Margaret Douglas, to join the English court around 1530. At the age of 15, she was originally housed with her aunt, Mary Tudor, and then joined the household of Henry's daughter, the Princess Mary, whom she would be friends with for life. As Henry's marital relationships changed, she served under Queen Anne Boleyn where it was noted he treated her like a queen's daughter[2] and Anne of Cleves.

After Margaret's first stint in the tower for her betrothal to Thomas Howard, she fell in love with Charles Howard, the brother of Catherine Howard, Henry's fifth wife. Their relationship only came to light during Catherine Howard's downfall. Her beloved Charles fled to Flanders whilst Privy councillors were instructed to 'first declare unto her how indiscreetly she hath demeaned herself towards the King's majesty, first with the Lord Thomas, and secondly with the Lord Charles Howard; in which part, you shall by discretion, charge her with overmuch lightness, and, finally, give her advice to beware the third time, and wholly apply herself to please the King's Majesty, and to follow and obey that shall be his Highness' will and commandment, with other such exhortations as good advices as by your wisdom you can devise to that purpose'.[3] After her utter dressing-down, Margaret was sent to live at Kenninghall under the supervision of Lord Norfolk. She was received back at court in 1543 to wait upon Catherine Parr, Henry's sixth and final wife.

Matthew Stewart, Earl of Lennox, was descended from James II and as such had a claim to the Scottish throne. He contested Arran's regency and plotted to marry either Marie de Guise or Margaret Douglas to strengthen his claim. Henry was initially happy for him to marry Margaret, seeing him as an ally who he could control but became wary of him after he raised 10,000 men to remove Mary, Queen of Scots from Arran's hold. Henry would put conditions on the marriage between Lennox and his niece to ensure his fidelity and with this organised Margaret was married at St James's Palace on 29 June 1544.

Margaret's father, the Earl of Angus, was not at the wedding, He had continued to work for Henry after Margaret Tudor's death but after the 'Rough Wooing' – a period of hostile English forays into Scotland that included the devastation of Angus's own lands – he turned back to supporting the Scottish crown. As Margaret Tudor had once been caught between her husband and her brother, her daughter would be caught between her husband and her father. For now her allegiance must remain with England. After her marriage she remained at court as Catherine Parr's lady. Lennox was often away sent on campaign into Scotland by the king but come the start of the new year, she was confined at Stepney Palace for the birth of her first son, Henry Stewart, Lord Darnley in February 1545. Unfortunately he only lived for nine months.

During her time away her husband had been sent to charge her father with ingratitude to the king. Angus tried to placate Henry by saying he loved the King best of all men and as his daughter's husband, he loved Lennox entirely. He asked for a two-month truce but it was a stalling tactic as Angus was in charge at the battle of Ancrum Moor where the Scots defeated the English troops. Margaret's relationship with her father would forever after be fraught.

Away from all the politics Margaret gave birth to her next son, also named Henry early in December 1546 at her estate at Temple Newsam in Yorkshire granted to the couple by her uncle, Henry VIII. A soothsayer told her that this son would be king of England and Scotland and she certainly held on to that prophecy as he was growing up. The English king was now ailing and on 28 January 1547 he died at Whitehall. Margaret was left out of the succession and Prince Edward was crowned at nine years of age. There was no place for Margaret at his court, there was no queen to serve and Edward's dislike of Catholics put her in an awkward position. Lennox continued to serve the new king as Margaret concentrated on raising her family but her son's rise was never far from her mind.

As the years passed, Lennox spent more time with Margaret, outlawed in Scotland, he took to running his estates and when a peace treaty was signed between England and Scotland in 1551 he was no longer needed by King Edward. Margaret however was called to court to welcome Marie de Guise on her visit to London. Not long after her father asked her to visit him at Tantallon and after some prevarication by Edward's councillors, she was eventually granted permission to go to Scotland for two months providing her husband and children stayed in England. It was the last time she would see him and although their relationship in later years had been troublesome, his death in January 1557 caused her much sorrow.

Margaret was back at court and high in favour during Mary I's reign. Friends since childhood, the two women shared the same religion and many stories from their younger days but Mary's turn as a Tudor monarch only lasted five years. She had hoped the succession would finally pass to Margaret but instead it was her younger sister, Elizabeth, who would take the crown. Margaret had never been close to Anne Boleyn's daughter but she immediately set out to make a good impression.

Congratulating the new queen, Margaret hoped to continue as first lady at court. She took part in Elizabeth's state entry into London but it seems that was all she was needed for. The new queen did not give her a position and she returned to her estates at Temple Newsam and Settrington. She was not trusted. Margaret had been too close to Mary and being of royal blood, was also a threat to Elizabeth's crown. The young Tudor queen tried to have Margaret declared illegitimate thus taking her out of any succession and removing her claim to the throne, but although her father had been pre-contracted to marry another woman, it did not render her mother's marriage invalid and the pope had declared her legitimate. Margaret in turn didn't think much of Elizabeth's legitimacy either.

But Elizabeth was right not to trust Margaret. The Countess of Lennox was plotting to elevate her family. Marie de Guise had eventually become regent of Scotland but she died in June 1560. In the same year, the French dauphin, now King Francis II, died leaving her daughter Mary a widow at the age of eighteen. Margaret thought it would be an excellent idea for her son to marry his cousin. In fact, she had worked for several years to bring Darnley to Mary's attention, sending him to France with condolences after Henri II's death in July 1559 and again after Francis's death.

The English queen, who had kept the Lennox household under surveillance and heard of Margaret's plotting, sent her husband to the Tower and placed Margaret under house arrest in 1562. Margaret was accused of 15 offences including treason and witchcraft but maintained she was innocent of all. Eventually Elizabeth allowed Lennox to join his wife at Sheen for a time before they were freed on condition they would not allow Darnley to marry without the queen's consent. Margaret returned to Settringham but before long she was recalled to court with her son. Elizabeth felt her plotting could be kept under control if the countess and Darnley were where she could see them and she seemed to genuinely have some affection for Darnley, a young, attractive youth, who amused her and played the lute for her in the evenings.

When Mary, Queen of Scots, back in power in Scotland, agreed to restore Lennox's family property and lift his ban on entering Scotland, Margaret's husband asked Elizabeth's permission to travel north. The queen at first refused but then allowed him to go as long as he did nothing to ferment anti-English feeling. Mary then asked for Darnley and again Elizabeth refused but in January 1565 she allowed him to go for three months. Margaret was obliged to stay at court as much as she wanted to go to Scotland with her family and she was comfortable enough there until Mary sent a message to Elizabeth asking for permission to marry her son. This was a step too far for the English queen. Darnley, as her subject, should have asked himself. Elizabeth took it out on Margaret who was now confined to her chamber at Whitehall and she sent a message to Lennox and Darnley to return to court immediately which they ignored. Margaret then found herself back in the Tower. Lennox, Darnley and Mary all appealed for her release but Elizabeth was furious at them all. Margaret was alone and in peril but her plan had worked. On 29 July 1565, Mary, Queen of Scots married her 18-year-old son at Holyrood.

But the marriage was not a happy one. Darnley had fluctu-ating moods, drank too much, craved power and was extremely jealous of Mary's Italian private secretary, David Rizzio. Rizzio had first come to Mary's attention singing with a French quartet to entertain the court. She liked him so much he was made gentleman of the privy chamber and rose to become her secretary in 1564 before her marriage to Darnley. Many Scottish nobles resented his closeness to the queen, especially her husband, and rumours abounded that he was far too intimate with her. Darnley even went as far as accusing her of being the father of the child she was carrying.

On 9 March 1566 Darnley burst into her rooms with a band of his loyal men. Grabbing Mary to one side, the men stabbed Rizzio 56 times in front of her. Although Darnley had not wielded a dagger Mary railed at him for arranging her secretary's death 'it is sayde that he dyd answer, that David had more companie of her body than he... and therefore, for her honor and his owne contentement he gave his consent that he should be taken away'.[4] What relationship Mary and Darnley had was now fractured.

Mary's son Charles James was born on 19 June 1566 at Edinburgh Castle. He was baptised in a Catholic ceremony on 17 December 1566 at Stirling Castle. Elizabeth I was one of his godparents as were Charles IX of France and Emmanuel Philibert, Duke of Savoy. Darnley refused to attend the ceremony, still maintaining the child was Rizzio's. Margaret, still in the Tower, despaired of her son and asked Silva, the Spanish ambassador, 'to make very effort to bring them into harmony again'.[5]

The Scots disliked Darnley, feeling he had become too power hungry, and the following February, an explosion was heard echoing across Edinburgh. The house at Kirk o' Field where he was staying erupted with flame. It was later discovered that two barrels of gunpowder had been set under Darnley's bedchamber. He was found with his valet dead in the orchard. Rather than showing signs of being in the explosion it looked like they had been murdered beforehand by strangulation.

When the news reached the English court, Elizabeth knew Margaret had to be told. She sent Margaret Gamage, Lord Howard's wife, and Mildred Cooke, Cecil's wife, to inform her that her son and her husband were dead. The news that Lennox was dead was wrong but believed at the time. Later, Cecil was able to confirm that at least her husband was still alive but Margaret was devastated. Her golden boy, the one she had pinned all her hopes and dreams on, was dead at the young age of 20, and she blamed Mary for his death. It was reported 'she is not the only person that suspects the Queen to have had some hand in the business, and they think they see in it revenge for her Italian secretary, and the long estrangement which this caused between her and her husband'.[6] Others pointed the finger Elizabeth's way.

Margaret was released from the Tower and allowed to reside at Sackville Place with her younger son, Charles. Darnley had already been buried at Holyrood so there was no need to travel to Scotland even if Elizabeth had allowed it. Her husband had sworn to stay on there to bring their son's murderers to justice. Lennox believed it was Bothwell and urged the Queen of Scots to move against him. James Hepburn, 4th Earl of Bothwell, was acquitted of the charge in April 1567 but to add more fuel to the rumours, he married Mary soon after. There is some debate about how willing Mary was. She was waylaid on her return from visiting her son at Stirling and taken to Dunbar Castle where Bothwell supposedly raped her, forcing her to marry him. Many thought it was an excuse to cover up their true relationship.

Although Bothwell had many followers, he had reached too far in his aim for power. Many Scottish lords rose against the couple and their troops met each other on 15 June 1567 at Carberry Hill. Bothwell fled the field and Mary was forced to surrender and imprisoned in Lochleven Castle. She had lost any authority she once had after Darnley's death and her association with Bothwell. Mary, Queen of Scots, was forced to abdicate on 24 July 1567 in favour of her son now James VI, King of Scotland, and to appoint her illegitimate half-brother, James Stewart, Earl of Moray, as regent.

There was some talk of Margaret's grandson being brought up in England but it was not to be. Moray acted as his regent until his assassination in 1570. Lennox took over the role but he too fell prey to opposing political forces and was shot in a skirmish the following year when men loyal to Mary attacked Stirling. He made it back to the castle but later died of a stomach wound. With his dying breath, he sent his love to his wife.

Margaret was told the sad news by Elizabeth. She had no one left except her younger son Charles and she now turned her attentions to him. In another fateful move she arranged his marriage with Elizabeth Cavendish, daughter of Bess of Hardwick, Countess of Shrewsbury. Both mothers contrived for their children to meet and secretly wed in Rufford Abbey in November 1574 without the queen's permission. What were they thinking? They both knew how Elizabeth reacted when she felt threatened and the joining of this couple would be seen as another threat to her crown. It should have been no surprise when Margaret, her son and daughter-in-law were summoned to court to answer for their actions. Bess of Hardwick was placed under house arrest. Charles and his wife were split up and Margaret found herself, once again, in the Tower. Elizabeth was convinced the marriage was part of a larger plot involving Mary, Queen of Scots, but her councillors could find no evidence for it. Margaret was released in March 1575.

The newly wedded couple had returned to Bess's home at Chatsworth where Elizabeth gave birth to Margaret's granddaughter, Arbella, later in the year. Margaret spent much time with them until Charles' death in April 1576 at just 19 years of age. The daughter of Margaret Tudor was in her sixties when two years later after a short illness she died at her house in Hackney after living as much of a tumultuous life as her mother had done.

Mary's subsequent escape from Scotland, her continuing relationship with Elizabeth once in England and her demise at Fotheringhay Castle on 8 February 1587 is well documented. The English queen lived until 1603 and it is here that Margaret Tudor's legacy finally came to pass in the joining of her two countries, England and Scotland. James VI, Margaret's great grandson, was king of Scotland but succeeded Elizabeth as king of England and Ireland as James I on 24 March 1603. So Margaret's great grandson finally accomplished what she had hoped for all her life and that was to join Scotland and England in harmony.

References

Chapter One: The Early Years 1489–1502

1. Leland, *De Rebus Brittanicis Collectanea Vol 5*, London, 1774
2. Green, Mary Anne Everett, *Lives of the Princesses of England from the Norman Conquest*, London, 1857
3. Strickland, Agnes, *Lives of the Tudor Princesses*, London, 1868
4. Buchanan, Patricia, *Margaret Tudor Queen of Scots*, Edinburgh, 1985
5. Vergil, Polydore, *Anglica Historia, A hypertext critical edition*, ed. Sutton, Dana F, Irvine, 2005
6. CSP Spain
7. Green, Mary Anne Everett, *Lives of the Princesses of England from the Norman Conquest*, London, 1857
8. Leland, *De Rebus Brittanicis Collectanea Vol 5*, London, 1774
9. Green, Mary Anne Everett, *Lives of the Princesses of England from the Norman Conquest*, London, 1857
10. Harvey, Nancy Lenz, *The Rose and the Thorn*, New York, 1975
11. Ibid.
12. Green, Mary Anne Everett, *Lives of the Princesses of England from the Norman Conquest*, London, 1857
13. Ibid.
14. Leland, *De Rebus Brittanicis Collectanea Vol 5*, London, 1774
15. Aleyn, George, *The Historie Of Henrie The Seventh*
16. Leland, *De Rebus Brittanicis Collectanea Vol 5*, London, 1774
17. Ibid.
18. Ibid.
19. CSP Spain
20. Weir, Alison, *The Six Wives of Henry VIII*, London, 1991
21. Leland, *De Rebus Brittanicis Collectanea Vol 5*, London, 1774

Chapter Two: Marriage to James IV 1503

1. More, Sir Thomas, *The Complete Works of Sir Thomas More*,

New Haven, 1963-97

2. Green, Mary Anne Everett, *Lives of the Princesses of England from the Norman Conquest*, London, 1857

3. Routh, EMG, *Lady Margaret*, Oxford, 1924

4. Strickland, Agnes, *Lives of the Tudor Princesses*, London, 1868

5. Leland, *De Rebus Brittanicis Collectanea Vol 5*, London, 1774

6. Ibid.

7. Ibid.

8. Ibid.

9. Yonge, John, 'The Fyancells of Margaret, Eledest Daughter of Henry VII', in Leland, *Collectenea*, Vol IV. Edited by Thomas Hearne, Oxford 1710-1712

10. Ibid.

11. Ibid.

12. Ibid.

13. Harvey, Nancy Lenz, *The Rose and the Thorn*, New York, 1975

14. Green, Mary Anne Everett, *Lives of the Princesses of England from the Norman Conquest*, London, 1857

15. Leland, *De Rebus Brittanicis Collectanea Vol 5*, London, 1774

16. Ibid.

17. Ibid.

18. Green, Mary Anne Everett, *Lives of the Princesses of England from the Norman Conquest*, London, 1857

19. Ibid.

20. Leland, *De Rebus Brittanicis Collectanea Vol 5*, London, 1774

21. Ibid.

22. Ibid.

23. Green, Mary Anne Everett, *Lives of the Princesses of England from the Norman Conquest*, London, 1857

24. Ibid.

25. Ibid.

Chapter Three: Queen of Scotland 1504–1512

1. Lesley, Bishop, *History of Scotland*, Edinburgh, 1829

2. Dunbar, William, *Poems*, Oxford, 1958
3. Ibid.
4. Green, Mary Anne Everett, *Lives of the Princesses of England from the Norman Conquest*, London, 1857
5. Lesley, Bishop, History of Scotland, Edinburgh, 1829
6. Buchanan, Patricia, *Margaret Tudor Queen of Scots*, Edinburgh, 1985
7. Green, Mary Anne Everett, *Lives of the Princesses of England from the Norman Conquest*, London, 1857
8. Buchanan, Patricia, *Margaret Tudor Queen of Scots*, Edinburgh, 1985
9. Perry, Maria, *Sisters to the King*, London, 1998
10. Goodwin, George, *Fatal Rivalry: Flodden 1513*, London, 2013
11. Buchanan, Patricia, *Margaret Tudor Queen of Scots*, Edinburgh, 1985
12. Hutchinson, Robert, *Young Henry: The Rise of Henry VIII*, London, 2011
13. Harvey, Nancy Lenz, *The Rose and the Thorn*, New York, 1975
14. Green, Mary Anne Everett, *Lives of the Princesses of England from the Norman Conquest*, London, 1857
15. Green, Mary Anne Everett, *Lives of the Princesses of England from the Norman Conquest*, London, 1857
16. Dunbar, William, *Poems*, Oxford, 1958
17. Anon, *Sir Andrew Barton*, accessed http://www.poemhunter.com/poem/sir-andrew-barton/
18. Hall, Edward, *Hall's Chronicle: Containing the history of England,* ed. H. Ellis, London, 1809
19. Chapman, Hester, *The Sisters of Henry VIII*, Bath, 1969
20. Lindsay, R, *History and Chronicles of Scotland*, Edinburgh, 1814
21. Ibid.
22. Green, Mary Anne Everett, *Lives of the Princesses of England from the Norman Conquest*, London, 1857
23. Ibid.
24. Ibid.

25. *Letters and Papers, Foreign and Domestic, Henry VIII*
26. Taylor, IA, *The Life of James IV*, London, 1913

Chapter Four: Flodden and its Aftermath 1513–1514

1.   *Letters and Papers, Foreign and Domestic, Henry VIII*
2.   Ibid.
3.   Chapman, Hester, *The Sisters of Henry VIII*, Bath, 1969
4.   Buchanan, Patricia, *Margaret Tudor Queen of Scots*, Edinburgh, 1985
5.   *Letters and Papers, Foreign and Domestic, Henry VIII*
6.   Ibid.
7.   Ibid.
8.   Green, Mary Anne Everett, *Lives of the Princesses of England from the Norman Conquest*, London, 1857
9.   *Letters and Papers, Foreign and Domestic, Henry VIII*
10. Ibid.
11. *Letters and Papers, Foreign and Domestic, Henry VIII*
12. Buchanan, Patricia, *Margaret Tudor Queen of Scots*, Edinburgh, 1985
13. Ibid.
14. Ibid.
15. Chapman, Hester, *The Sisters of Henry VIII*, Bath, 1969
16. Hall, Edward, *Hall's Chronicle: Containing the history of England*, ed. H. Ellis, London, 1809
17. Hutchinson, Robert, *House of Treason: The Rise and Fall of a Tudor Dynasty*, London, 2009
18. Drummond, W, *History of Scotland*, London, 1745
19. Ibid.
20. *Letters and Papers, Foreign and Domestic, Henry VIII*
21. Ibid.
22. Drummond, W, *History of Scotland*, London, 1745
23. Buchanan, Patricia, *Margaret Tudor Queen of Scots*, Edinburgh, 1985
24. Green, Mary Anne Everett, *Lives of the Princesses of England*

from the Norman Conquest, London, 1857

25. Drummond, W, *History of Scotland*, London, 1745
26. Hall, Edward, *Hall's Chronicle: Containing the history of England,* ed. H. Ellis, London, 1809
27. Green, Mary Anne Everett, *Lives of the Princesses of England from the Norman Conquest*, London, 1857
28. Perry, Maria, *Sisters to the King,* London, 1998
29. Green, Mary Anne Everett, *Lives of the Princesses of England from the Norman Conquest*, London, 1857
30. Perry, Maria, *Sisters to the King,* London, 1998
31. *Letters and Papers, Foreign and Domestic, Henry VIII*
32. Green, Mary Anne Everett, *Lives of the Princesses of England from the Norman Conquest*, London, 1857
33. Lindsay, R, *History and Chronicles of Scotland*, Edinburgh, 1814
34. Strickland, Agnes, *Lives of the Tudor Princesses*, London, 1868
35. Buchanan, Patricia, *Margaret Tudor Queen of Scots*, Edinburgh, 1985
36. Green, Mary Anne Everett, *Letters of Royal and Illustrious Ladies of Great Britain*, London, 1846

Chapter Five: A New Regency 1515–1516

1. Green, Mary Anne Everett, *Letters of Royal and Illustrious Ladies of Great Britain*, London, 1846
2. Green, Mary Anne Everett, *Lives of the Princesses of England from the Norman Conquest*, London, 1857
3. Ibid.
4. Ibid.
5. Chapman, Hester, *The Sisters of Henry VIII*, Bath, 1969
6. Harvey, Nancy Lenz, *The Rose and the Thorn*, New York, 1975
7. Perry, Maria, *Sisters to the King,* London, 1998
8. Green, Mary Anne Everett, *Lives of the Princesses of England from the Norman Conquest*, London, 1857
9. Harvey, Nancy Lenz, *The Rose and the Thorn*, New York, 1975
10. Strickland, Agnes, *Lives of the Tudor Princesses*, London, 1868

11. Green, Mary Anne Everett, *Letters of Royal and Illustrious Ladies of Great Britain*, London, 1846

12. Green, Mary Anne Everett, *Lives of the Princesses of England from the Norman Conquest*, London, 1857

13. Chapman, Hester, *The Sisters of Henry VIII*, Bath, 1969

14. Buchanan, Patricia, *Margaret Tudor Queen of Scots*, Edinburgh, 1985

15. Green, Mary Anne Everett, *Lives of the Princesses of England from the Norman Conquest*, London, 1857

16. Ibid.

17. *Letters and Papers, Foreign and Domestic, Henry VIII*

18. Harvey, Nancy Lenz, *The Rose and the Thorn*, New York, 1975

19. Buchanan, Patricia, *Margaret Tudor Queen of Scots*, Edinburgh, 1985

20. Harvey, Nancy Lenz, *The Rose and the Thorn*, New York, 1975

21. Perry, Maria, *Sisters to the King*, London, 1998

22. Hall, Edward, *Hall's Chronicle: Containing the history of England*, ed. H. Ellis, London, 1809

23. Ibid.

24. *Letters and Papers, Foreign and Domestic, Henry VIII*

Chapter Six: Return to Scotland 1517

1. Hall, Edward, *Hall's Chronicle: Containing the history of England*, ed. H. Ellis, London, 1809

2. Chapman, Hester, *The Sisters of Henry VIII*, Bath, 1969

3. Buchanan, Patricia, *Margaret Tudor Queen of Scots*, Edinburgh, 1985

4. Green, Mary Anne Everett, *Lives of the Princesses of England from the Norman Conquest*, London, 1857

5. Buchanan, Patricia, *Margaret Tudor Queen of Scots*, Edinburgh, 1985

6. Green, Mary Anne Everett, *Letters of Royal and Illustrious Ladies of Great Britain*, London, 1846

7. Green, Mary Anne Everett, *Lives of the Princesses of England*

from the Norman Conquest, London, 1857

8. Green, Mary Anne Everett, *Letters of Royal and Illustrious Ladies of Great Britain*, London, 1846
9. Ibid.
10. Buchanan, Patricia, *Margaret Tudor Queen of Scots*, Edinburgh, 1985
11. Green, Mary Anne Everett, *Letters of Royal and Illustrious Ladies of Great Britain*, London, 1846
12. Green, Mary Anne Everett, *Lives of the Princesses of England from the Norman Conquest*, London, 1857
13. *Letters and Papers, Foreign and Domestic, Henry VIII*
14. Green, Mary Anne Everett, *Lives of the Princesses of England from the Norman Conquest*, London, 1857
15. Ibid.
16. Chapman, Hester, *The Sisters of Henry VIII*, Bath, 1969
17. *Letters and Papers, Foreign and Domestic, Henry VIII*
18. Green, Mary Anne Everett, *Letters of Royal and Illustrious Ladies of Great Britain*, London, 1846
19. Green, Mary Anne Everett, *Lives of the Princesses of England from the Norman Conquest*, London, 1857
20. Green, Mary Anne Everett, *Letters of Royal and Illustrious Ladies of Great Britain*, London, 1846
21. Ibid.

Chapter Seven: Enter the King 1522–1523

1. Perry, Maria, *Sisters to the King*, London, 1998
2. Green, Mary Anne Everett, *Lives of the Princesses of England from the Norman Conquest*, London, 1857
3. Ibid.
4. Green, Mary Anne Everett, *Letters of Royal and Illustrious Ladies of Great Britain*, London, 1846
5. Lesley, Bishop, *History of Scotland*, Edinburgh, 1829
6. Chapman, Hester, *The Sisters of Henry VIII*, Bath, 1969
7. Buchanan, Patricia, *Margaret Tudor Queen of Scots*, Edinburgh,

1985

8. *Letters and Papers, Foreign and Domestic, Henry VIII*
9. Ibid.
10. Watkins, Sarah-Beth, *The Tudor Brandons*, Alresford, 2016
11. Buchanan, Patricia, *Margaret Tudor Queen of Scots*, Edinburgh, 1985
12. Green, Mary Anne Everett, *Letters of Royal and Illustrious Ladies of Great Britain*, London, 1846
13. Ibid.
14. Ibid.
15. Green, Mary Anne Everett, *Lives of the Princesses of England from the Norman Conquest*, London, 1857
16. Ibid.
17. Green, Mary Anne Everett, *Letters of Royal and Illustrious Ladies of Great Britain*, London, 1846
18. *Letters and Papers, Foreign and Domestic, Henry VIII*
19. Buchanan, Patricia, *Margaret Tudor Queen of Scots*, Edinburgh, 1985
20. Ibid.
21. Green, Mary Anne Everett, *Letters of Royal and Illustrious Ladies of Great Britain*, London, 1846
22. Green, Mary Anne Everett, *Lives of the Princesses of England from the Norman Conquest*, London, 1857

Chapter Eight: The Reign of James V 1524–1536

1. Green, Mary Anne Everett, *Lives of the Princesses of England from the Norman Conquest*, London, 1857
2. Ibid.
3. Strickland, Agnes, *Lives of the Tudor Princesses*, London, 1868
4. Green, Mary Anne Everett, *Lives of the Princesses of England from the Norman Conquest*, London, 1857
5. Ibid.
6. Chapman, Hester, *The Sisters of Henry VIII*, Bath, 1969
7. Perry, Maria, *Sisters to the King*, London, 1998

8.   Green, Mary Anne Everett, *Letters of Royal and Illustrious Ladies of Great Britain*, London, 1846

9.   Green, Mary Anne Everett, *Lives of the Princesses of England from the Norman Conquest*, London, 1857

10. Chapman, Hester, *The Sisters of Henry VIII*, Bath, 1969

11. Ibid.

12. Green, Mary Anne Everett, *Lives of the Princesses of England from the Norman Conquest*, London, 1857

13. Buchanan, Patricia, *Margaret Tudor Queen of Scots*, Edinburgh, 1985

14. Green, Mary Anne Everett, *Lives of the Princesses of England from the Norman Conquest*, London, 1857

15. Weir, Alison, *The Lost Tudor Princess: A Life of Margaret Douglas, Countess of Lennox*, London, 2016

16. Green, Mary Anne Everett, *Lives of the Princesses of England from the Norman Conquest*, London, 1857

17. Ibid.

18. Buchanan, Patricia, *Margaret Tudor Queen of Scots*, Edinburgh, 1985

19. Green, Mary Anne Everett, *Letters of Royal and Illustrious Ladies of Great Britain*, London, 1846

20. Chapman, Hester, *The Sisters of Henry VIII*, Bath, 1969

21. Perry, Maria, *Sisters to the King*, London, 1998

22. Green, Mary Anne Everett, *Letters of Royal and Illustrious Ladies of Great Britain*, London, 1846

Chapter Nine: The Final Years 1537–1541

1.   *Letters and Papers, Foreign and Domestic, Henry VIII*

2.   Bingham, Caroline, *James V: King of Scots*, London, 1971

3.   *Letters and Papers, Foreign and Domestic, Henry VIII*

4.   Chapman, Hester, *The Sisters of Henry VIII*, Bath, 1969

5.   Marshall, Rosalind Kay, *Mary of Guise*, London, 1977

6.   Bingham, Caroline, *James V: King of Scots*, London, 1971

7.   *Letters and Papers, Foreign and Domestic, Henry VIII*

8. Buchanan, Patricia, *Margaret Tudor Queen of Scots*, Edinburgh, 1985
9. Green, Mary Anne Everett, *Letters of Royal and Illustrious Ladies of Great Britain*, London, 1846

Chapter Ten: Margaret's Legacy

1. Bingham, Caroline, *James V: King of Scots*, London, 1971
2. Weir, Alison, *The Lost Tudor Princess: A Life of Margaret Douglas, Countess of Lennox*, London, 2016
3. Ibid.
4. Wright, Thomas (ed), *Queen Elizabeth and Her Times: A Series of Original Letters, Selected from the Inedited Private Correspondence of the Lord Treasurer Burghley, the Earl of Leicester, the Secretaries Walsingham and Smith, Sir Christopher Hatton, and Most of the Distinguished Persons of the Period, Volume 1*, London, 1838
5. Weir, Alison, *The Lost Tudor Princess: A Life of Margaret Douglas, Countess of Lennox*, London, 2016
6. Ibid.

Select Bibliography

Anglo, Sydney, *The Court Festivals of Henry VII: A Study based upon the account books of John Heron, Treasurer of the Chamber,* Bulletin of the John Rylands Library 43, 1960-61

Arthurson, Ian, *The Perkin Warbeck Conspiracy,* London, 2009

Bacon, Francis, *The History of the Reign of King Henry VII and Selected Works,* Cambridge, 1998

Bernard, André, *The Life of Henry VII,* translated and introduced by Daniel Hobbins, New York, 2011

Bernard, G W, *The Tudor Nobility,* Manchester, 1992

Bingham, Caroline, *James V: King of Scots,* London, 1971

Borland, Robert, *Border Raids and Reivers,* London, 1989

Bruce, Marie Louise, *The Making of Henry VIII,* London, 1977

Buchanan, Patricia, *Margaret Tudor Queen of Scots,* Edinburgh, 1985

Calendar of State Papers, France

Calendar of State Papers, Scotland

Cavendish, George, *The Life and Death of Cardinal Wolsey,* Massachusetts, 1905

Chapman, Hester, *The Sisters of Henry VIII,* Bath, 1969

Drummond, W, *History of Scotland,* London, 1745

Dunbar, William, *Poems,* Oxford, 1958

Erickson, Carolly, *Great Harry: The Extravagant Life of Henry VIII,* London, 1997

Green, Mary Anne Everett, *Letters of Royal and Illustrious Ladies of Great Britain,* London, 1846

Green, Mary Anne Everett, *Lives of the Princesses of England from the Norman Conquest,* London, 1857

Fraser, Antonia, *The Six Wives of Henry VIII,* London, 1992

Gardiner, J, ed, *Memorials of King Henry VII,* London, 1858

Glenne, Michael, *King Harry's Sister,* London, 1952

Griffiths, R A, *The Making of the Tudor Dynasty,* Stroud, 2011

Goodwin, George, *Fatal Rivalry: Flodden 1513*, London, 2013

Hall, Edward, *Hall's Chronicle: Containing the history of England*, ed. H. Ellis, London, 1809

Harvey, Nancy Lenz, *The Rose and the Thorn*, New York, 1975

Holinshed, Raphael, *Chronicles of England, Scotland and Ireland*, London, 1807

Hutchinson, Robert, *House of Treason: The Rise and Fall of a Tudor Dynasty*, London, 2009

Hutchinson, Robert, *Young Henry: The Rise of Henry VIII*, London, 2011

Leland, *De Rebus Brittanicis Collectanea Vol 5*, London, 1774

Lesley, Bishop, *History of Scotland*, Edinburgh, 1829

Letters and Papers, Foreign and Domestic, Henry VIII

Licence, Amy, *Elizabeth of York*, Stroud, 2014

Lindsay, R, *History and Chronicles of Scotland*, Edinburgh, 1814

Loades, David, *Henry VIII: Court, church and conflict*, The National Archives, 2007

Loads, David, *Henry VIII: King and Court*, Andover, 2009

Macdougall, Norman, *James IV*, Edinburgh, 1989

Mackay, Lauren, *Inside the Tudor Court*, Stroud, 2014

Marshall, Rosalind Kay, *Mary of Guise*, London, 1977

Mathusiak, John, *Henry VIII*, Stroud, 2013

Mathusiak, John, *Wolsey*, Stroud, 2014

Merriman, RB, *Life and Letters of Thomas Cromwell*, Oxford, 1902

More, Sir Thomas, *The Complete Works of Sir Thomas More*, New Haven, 1963-97

Mumby, Frank Arthur, *The Youth of Henry VIII: A Narrative in Contemporary Letters*, London, 1913

Nichols, John Gough, *The Chronicle of Calais, in the reigns of Henry VII and Henry VIII to the year 1540*, J. B. Nichols and Son, 1846

Parmiter, Geoffrey de C, *The King's Great Matter*, London, 1967

Perry, Maria, *Sisters to the King*, London, 1998

Rogers, E, ed, *Correspondence of Thomas More*, Princeton, 1947

Routh, EMG, *Lady Margaret*, Oxford, 1924

Royle, Trevor, *The Road to Bosworth Field*, London, 2009

Scarisbrick, J J, *Henry VIII*, London, 1997

Seward, Desmond, *The Last White Rose*, London, 2011

Skidmore, Chris, *Bosworth: The Birth of the Tudors*, London, 2014

Smith, Gregory, *The Days of James IV*, Createspace, 2016

Soberton, Sylvia Barbara, *The Forgotten Tudor Women*, Great Britain, 2015

Starkey, David, *Henry, Virtuous Prince*, London, 2009

Starkey, David, *The Reign of Henry VIII*, London, 1985

Starkey, David, *Six Wives: The Queens of Henry VIII*, London, 2003

Strickland, Agnes, *Lives of the Tudor Princesses*, London, 1868

Strype, *Ecclesiastical Memorials of Henry VIII, Edward VI and Mary*, London, 1816

Stuart, Marie W., *The Scot who was a Frenchman*, London, 1940

Taylor, IA, *The Life of James IV*, London, 1913

Thomas, A H and Thornley, I D, eds, *Great Chronicle of London*, London, 1938

Vergil, Polydore, *Anglica Historia, A hypertext critical edition*, ed. Sutton, Dana F, Irvine, 2005

Watkins, Sarah-Beth, *The Tudor Brandons*, Alresford, 2016

Weir, Alison, *Elizabeth of York: The First Tudor Queen*, London, 2014

Weir, Alison, *Henry VIII: King and Court*, London, 2008

Weir, Alison, *The Six Wives of Henry VIII*, London, 1991

Weir, Alison, *The Lost Tudor Princess: A Life of Margaret Douglas, Countess of Lennox*, London, 2016

Wright, Thomas (ed), *Queen Elizabeth and Her Times: A Series of Original Letters, Selected from the Inedited Private Correspondence of the Lord Treasurer Burghley, the Earl of Leicester, the Secretaries Walsingham and Smith, Sir Christopher Hatton, and Most of the Distinguished Persons of the Period, Volume 1*, London, 1838

Yonge, John, 'The Fyancells of Margaret, Eldest Daughter of Henry VII', in Leland, *Collectenea*, Vol IV. Edited by Thomas Hearne, Oxford 1710-1712

Chronos Books
HISTORY

Chronos Books is an historical non-fiction imprint. Chronos
publishes real history for real people; bringing to life people,
places and events in an imaginative, easy-to-digest and
accessible way - histories that pass on their stories to a
generation of new readers.
If you have enjoyed this book, why not tell other readers by
posting a review on your preferred book site. Recent
bestsellers from Chronos Books are:

Lady Katherine Knollys
The Unacknowledged Daughter of King Henry VIII

Sarah-Beth Watkins
A comprehensive account of Katherine Knollys' questionable
paternity, her previously unexplored life in the Tudor court and
her intriguing relationship with Elizabeth I.
Paperback: 978-1-78279-585-8 ebook: 978-1-78279-584-1

Cromwell was Framed
Ireland 1649

Tom Reilly
Revealed: The definitive research that proves the Irish nation
owes Oliver Cromwell a huge posthumous apology for wrongly
convicting him of civilian atrocities in 1649.
Paperback: 978-1-78279-516-2 ebook: 978-1-78279-515-5

Why The CIA Killed JFK and Malcolm X
The Secret Drug Trade in Laos

John Koerner
A new groundbreaking work presenting evidence that the CIA
silenced JFK to protect its secret drug trade in Laos.
Paperback: 978-1-78279-701-2 ebook: 978-1-78279-700-5

The Disappearing Ninth Legion
A Popular History

Mark Olly
The Disappearing Ninth Legion examines hard evidence for the
foundation, development, mysterious disappearance, or possible
continuation of Rome's lost Legion.
Paperback: 978-1-84694-559-5 ebook: 978-1-84694-931-9

Beaten But Not Defeated
Siegfried Moos - A German anti-Nazi who settled in Britain

Merilyn Moos
Siegi Moos, an anti-Nazi and active member of the German
Communist Party, escaped Germany in 1933 and, exiled in
Britain, sought another route to the transformation of
capitalism.
Paperback: 978-1-78279-677-0 ebook: 978-1-78279-676-3

A Schoolboy's Wartime Letters
An evacuee's life in WWII — A Personal Memoir

Geoffrey Iley
A boy writes home during WWII, revealing his own fascinating
story, full of zest for life, information and humour.
Paperback: 978-1-78279-504-9 ebook: 978-1-78279-503-2

The Life & Times of the Real Robyn Hoode
Mark Olly
A journey of discovery. The chronicles of the genuine historical
character, Robyn Hoode, and how he became one of England's
greatest legends.
Paperback: 978-1-78535-059-7 ebook: 978-1-78535-060-3

Readers of ebooks can buy or view any of these bestsellers by
clicking on the live link in the title. Most titles are published
in paperback and as an ebook. Paperbacks are available in
traditional bookshops. Both print and ebook formats are
available online.

Find more titles and sign up to our readers' newsletter at
http://www.johnhuntpublishing.com/history-home

Follow us on Facebook at
https://www.facebook.com/ChronosBooks

and Twitter at https://twitter.com/ChronosBooks